CITYSPOTS
LJUBLJANA

Ryan Levitt

GW00375226

Written by Ryan Levitt
Updated by Marjorie Cunningham & Floor Tuinstra

Published by Thomas Cook Publishing
A division of Thomas Cook Tour Operations Limited
Company registration No: 1450464 England
The Thomas Cook Business Park, 9 Coningsby Road
Peterborough PE3 8SB, United Kingdom
Email: books@thomascook.com, Tel: +44 (0)1733 416477
www.thomascookpublishing.com

Produced by The Content Works Ltd
Aston Court, Kingsmead Business Park, Frederick Place
High Wycombe, Bucks HP11 1LA
www.thecontentworks.com

Series design based on an original concept by Studio 183 Limited

ISBN: 978-1-84157- 963-4

First edition © 2006 Thomas Cook Publishing
This second edition © 2008 Thomas Cook Publishing
Text © Thomas Cook Publishing
Maps © Thomas Cook Publishing/PCGraphics (UK) Limited
Transport map © Communicarta Limited

Series Editor: Kelly Anne Pipes
Production/DTP: Steven Collins

Printed and bound in Spain by GraphyCems

Cover photography (Robbov Fountain) © Jon Arnold/Alamy

CONTENTS

SYMBOLS KEY

The following symbols are used throughout this book:

ⓐ address ☏ telephone ⓦ website address ⓔ email
🕒 opening times Ⓝ public transport connections

The following symbols are used on the maps:

𝒊	information office	▪	points of interest
✈	airport	◯	city
➕	hospital	◯	large town
Ⓞ	police station	○	small town
🚍	bus station	═	motorway
🚇	railway station	—	main road
✝	cathedral	—	minor road
❶	numbers denote featured	—	railway
	cafés & restaurants		

Hotels and restaurants are graded by approximate price as follows:
£ budget price ££ mid-range price £££ expensive

▶ *Ljubljana Castle stands tall above the city*

INTRODUCING
Ljubljana

Introduction

While it may not be an influential capital like London, nor a sight-filled city like Paris, the Slovenian capital of Ljubljana is generating a lot of buzz among travellers, due to its streets of quaint charm, blossoming design and natural beauty. Low-cost airlines have blown the door wide open for holidaymakers searching for a city break destination that combines affordability, intriguing history, great food and stunning surroundings. Ljubljana offers all this and more.

While shoppers may find the options a tad on the disappointing side, locals would never want you to spend your time exploring stuffy boutiques. Instead, they will point you to the banks of the Ljubljanica River, where residents enjoy nothing more than a leisurely stroll as they watch the water flow by.

A visit to Ljubljana is made for those who want to relax. You won't need any strict itineraries or tight transport schedules to get the most out of your stay, as the city is so compact. To go from one end of Ljubljana to the other should take you no more than 45 minutes on foot – and that's if you walk at a slow pace.

Don't be at all worried that the small size might translate into a boring time – Slovenians are some of the friendliest and most welcoming people on the continent. If they think you're looking a bit down-hearted, they'll be sure to invite you to join their group in order to ensure that you experience a bit of true local hospitality.

Lovers of the great outdoors are especially well catered for, as Ljubljana is surrounded by huge tracts of untouched land. A large chunk of the western half of the city is devoted to the paths and fields of Tivoli Park, while a mere hour's drive outside town will take you to anything from the Alps to a fairytale lake complete with a castle overlooking its banks.

Ljubljana might be hard to say, but with all these options, your travel agent is sure to get used to saying its name as you book your stay again and again. Start saving your euros today!

⬥ *The narrow streets of the Old Town are perfect for exploring*

When to go

Ljubljana is worth visiting at any time of year. For many, the city really comes alive in the summer, when one outdoor event follows the next (see below), whether it is a colourful parade, street festival or an open-air concert. If what goes on in the city itself is not enough, then head off into the surroundings: the lake and castle of Bled (see page 102), the seafront at Piran (see page 120), and the fresh air of the Julian Alps are all enticing.

SEASONS & CLIMATE

Ljubljana has a continental climate, hot in summer and cold in winter. From November to March the city often ices over, with spring thawing everything out some time in late March and early April. Though the atmosphere is often quite damp, the temperatures are pleasant enough to allow outdoor activities such as walking and cycling.

Summers can be hot and muggy, and at this time of the year the locals flock to the shade of Tivoli (see page 92) or nearby Lake Bled (see page 102). In early autumn, temperatures are still very mild and, like spring, this is a good time to explore the city's streets. In winter, temperatures can drop fast and sudden snowstorms occasionally occur. Wrap up warmly and drop into the bars of the city which are sure to heat any chill.

ANNUAL EVENTS

In Ljubljana, and Slovenia in general, there are many more events than can be mentioned here. The tourist office in Ljubljana (see page 153) and the various regional capitals can provide a list of

● *Sparkling lights and reflections in Ljubljana at Christmas*

events. Also note that exact dates may change from year to year – check first. There is a comprehensive calendar of events at Ⓦ www.ljubljana-tourism.si/en

May
Druga Godba Ljubljana (late May) A week of concerts around the city that presents the best opportunity to experience and enjoy Slovenian folk and traditional music. Ⓦ www.drugagodba.si

June
Ana Desetnica Street Theatre Festival (late June) A colourful collection of performances that takes over the Old Town and highlights acts of magic and music.

Ljubljana Jazz Festival (late June) World-class musicians are often included on the bill of this three-day celebration of jazz and urban music. Ⓐ Krizanke Theatre, Trg francoske revolucije 1 Ⓦ www.ljubljanajazz.si

June–September
Ljubljana Summer Festival International music, theatre and dance performances, often in the strangest of venues (see web site for details). Ⓦ www.ljubljanafestival.si

August
TrnFest Ljubljana This month-long, hot-ticket arts event offers up workshops, guest lectures, small-scale performances and exhibitions organised by the KUD cultural centre (see page 91). Ⓦ www.kud-fp.si

September & October
International Biennial of Graphic Arts Held on odd-numbered years at the International Centre of Graphic Arts (the next is in 2009)

from September to October, this celebration of design is gaining in prestige among members of the global art community. **@** Grad Tivoli, Pod turnom 3 **ⓦ** www.mglc-lj.si/en

October
City of Women Art and culture created by women are the focus of this city-wide international festival of contemporary arts. **ⓦ** www.cityofwomen-a.si

December
Christmas Concerts Held in churches all over the city all month, these can be stunning.
Ljubljana's New Year's Eve Party Residents – and any visitors in town for the season of frivolity – congregate at Prešernov trg to take part in the celebrations.

PUBLIC HOLIDAYS
New Year's Holidays 1 & 2 Jan
Prešeren Day (Slovenian Culture Day) 8 Feb
Easter Sunday & Monday 12 & 13 Apr 2009; 4 & 5 Apr 2010
Insurrection Day 27 Apr
Labour Day Holidays 1 & 2 May
National Day 25 June
Assumption Day 15 Aug
Reformation Day 31 Oct
All Saints' Day 1 Nov
Christmas Day 25 Dec
Independence Day 26 Dec

Architectural opulence

The great thing about the architectural delights that are found in and around Ljubljana is that you don't have to be a connoisseur of art nouveau, baroque or Zopf in order to enjoy their beauty and diversity. All you require is the ability to be bowled over.

Art nouveau found glorious expression throughout Slovenia, and, in Ljubljana, it's the Left Bank area (see page 70) that possesses the most intriguing concentration of gems. Miklošičeva Cesta, the road that links Prešernov trg with the city's public transport stations, is considered to have the finest examples of art nouveau construction in town. Buildings to look out for include the Grand Hotel Union Executive (see page 37), the People's Loan Bank at number 4, the Cooperative Bank with its colourful geometric patterns at number 8, and the buildings that face Miklošičev Park. Just nearby, on Erjavčeva Cesta, the 1911 building that's now the home of the Slovenian National Drama Theatre (see page 83) is a captivating example of art nouveau, its interior almost a shrine to that genre's predilection for the curvilinear acanthus leaf motif.

But the Left Bank isn't all swirls and whiplash lines: Trg Republike, the district's main square, contains the Slovenian Parliament building (see page 74), a (to some) overblown burst of 1950s Eastern-bloc-style neoclassicism. It was designed by Vinko Glanz, an architect who was mightily influenced by Ljubljana's structural superstar, Jože Plečnik (see page 86). It was Ljubljana's National & University Library (see page 76) that cemented Plečnik's huge reputation. Interestingly, the Left Bank possesses a Plečnik vision that didn't come off: he decided to rebuild the original Roman wall that once circled the city, and the result is the stretch of wall that runs along the length of Mirje. It doesn't quite work, but it's an interesting concept nonetheless.

If you have a particular interest in architecture, do try to spend a few hours in Jože Plečnik's former abode, now Plečnik House & Collection (Ljubljana Architectural Museum, see page 86). He lived here from 1921 until his death in 1957, and it presents a fascinating insight into the workings of his inspired (and inspiring) mind. For an overview of where Slovenian architecture is at now, the DESSA Architectural Gallery (see page 75) will bring you up to speed on the city's current practitioners and trends.

Oh, yes – Zopf. Zopf was a transitional architectural style that bridged the gap between late baroque and neoclassicism in the early 18th century. The world's finest example of this is Ljubljana's Gruber Palace (see page 64).

⬤ *Plečnik's entrance gates to Žale Cemetery*

History

Ljubljana's history dates back to the Bronze Age. Inhabitants lived peacefully during these early days until the Celts moved southwards towards the Balkans from what is now France, Germany and the Czech Republic around 400 BC. The Roman Empire took over in 181 BC and established a number of regional colonies in order to ensure control over the area. Roman power was maintained until the 5th century AD when the Huns took advantage of the destruction of the Roman Empire.

The first Slavs to arrive in Slovenia came from the Carpathian basin and settled in the 6th century in the river valleys of Sava, Drava and Mura. These are the ancestors of today's Slovenians; however, the term 'Slovenian' didn't come into regular use until the 18th century.

Over the next 500 years, various clans, including the Franks, Magyars and Germans, ruled over the country, eventually culminating in the rise of the Habsburg family during the early Middle Ages. The Habsburgs ruled over Slovenia with an iron fist from the 14th century until the end of World War I. The laws of the land were administered by parliaments of princes, feudal lords and town representatives until the 17th century – however, all decisions needed to be approved by the Habsburgs.

Peasant uprisings caused problems for the Habsburgs at various times between the 14th and 19th centuries, as the gulf between the rich and poor continued to widen. Attacks from the south by Ottoman Turks fuelled rebellion as Slovenes were often left to fend for themselves during the deadly battles.

Protestantism entered the country as the Reformation swept across Europe. Determined to squash the revolutionary concepts introduced by this new branch of Christianity, the resident Catholic princes banished any believers from the country. This law didn't last long as state coffers began to reach breaking point. The Habsburgs battled to boost finances following years of ill-fated wars in other parts of the Empire. Roads were built, freedom of religion was reintroduced and corrupt Catholic orders were abolished.

The arrival of Napoleon brought new-found hope to Slovenia and initiated a period of Romantic Nationalism that would not be seen again until the independence movement of the early 1990s. The French general imposed a number of new reforms and allowed Slovene to be used in schools for the first time. These glory days didn't last for long as Austrian rule and the harsh feudal system were reintroduced in 1814.

World War I was the final nail in the coffin of Austrian rule. When the war ended, Slovenes joined together with Serbs and Croats to form the Independent Kingdom of Serbs, Croats and Slovenes. This unity was fragile, and faced ever stronger struggles following the introduction of Communism post-World War II. Were it not for the strong (if not dictatorial) rule of Tito, socialist Yugoslavia would never have survived. Finally, in 1991, after a ten-day war against Yugoslav forces, Slovenia gained independence. The country became a full member of the EU in May 2004 and, in 2007, became the first former communist bloc country to adopt the euro.

🔺 *Ljubljana Castle*

Lifestyle

The Germanic influences of the 600 years of Austro-German rule may explain the fact that Slovenians were considered the most efficient and formal people of the former Yugoslavia. However, the Slavic and Balkan blood provides a streak of humour that soon translates into a very warm welcome.

⬥ *Prešernov trg is the city's main square*

Residents are good business people and hard workers. The country was really the only one to emerge from the break-up of Yugoslavia relatively unscathed – primarily due to the nation's history as the region's financial hub.

Locals love a good time and have plenty of opportunities to indulge. While strong for the Balkans, the local economy isn't particularly booming, causing most residents to budget wisely. Admission costs to hip nightclubs are half those you'd expect in other major cities and drink prices are affordable. Speaking of nights out, a typical evening will start late: most clubs don't even open their doors until 23.00, and the funky and fashionable leave it another two hours before they even consider going inside. Bars are open (almost) all hours. Walk through most neighbourhoods and it is perfectly possible to find a bar open as late as 06.00. Locals enjoy a leisurely drinking culture and the company of friends.

Though there is a lack of big business in Ljubljana, this is starting to change as the city emerges as the powerhouse of the Balkans. A strong and individual community spirit survives as the city's biggest employers continue to be sole proprietors and independent companies. When someone says they work for a family-owned company in Ljubljana, that family has most likely owned the company for many generations.

Shopping isn't the all-consuming quasi-religion you find observed in Paris, London or New York. Hours reflect this trend, as the bulk of shops remain closed on Sundays and have severely restricted hours on Saturdays. Instead, it's a beer and a gossip that residents enjoy the most – preferably at an outdoor café on a warm summer evening. Winters can be harsh and locals value every minute of good weather. A public-place smoking ban was introduced in 2007, and this has extended the outside café culture long into the winter.

Culture

Ljubljana loves its artistic institutions. Public and private funding supports a number of theatres, concert halls, opera and ballet houses – both traditional and cutting-edge. Attendance at the various open-air theatres and concert venues explodes during the summer, when the city offers up a new festival almost every week – with most performances free of charge and open to all.

In warmer months, Prešernov trg is the place to go to enjoy live performance, whether in the form of rock acts, live swing bands, buskers or mimes. For a few euros more, walk a few blocks west to the **Cankarjev Dom** (ⓐ Vse pravice pridržane ⓘ (01) 241 7100 ⓦ www.cd-cc.si). This is the main performance venue in the city for big-name rock and classical acts. Acoustics are said to be superb. Philharmonic Hall (see page 83) is another venue worth booking tickets at, especially if the Slovenian Philharmonic Orchestra is scheduled to perform. The orchestra, one of the oldest in the world, was once conducted by the composer Gustav Mahler and continues to be widely respected. The Slovenian Chamber Choir also calls this venue home.

Diverse offerings can be found at the Križanke arts complex (see page 83) – a collection of open-air and intimate theatres housed in a converted 18th-century monastery. The grounds are also the headquarters of the annual Ljubljana Summer Festival (see page 10).

Squats and independent community centres are still widely accepted in Ljubljana, with local artists famous for transforming disused buildings into arts complexes, discos, bars and hostels. The most famous example of this is found at Metelkova (see page 82) and the **Hostel Celica** (ⓐ Metelkova 8 ⓘ (01) 230 9700

⬥ *The National Gallery holds many of Slovenia's art treasures*

Ⓦ www.souhostel.com), where a former army barracks and prison have been completely repainted and redesigned.

So why is Ljubljana so artistic? The country's status as a regional economic powerhouse provides one answer, especially when combined with new-found independence. For many years, the idea of a Slovenian identity was buried under layers of communism and Yugoslavian nationalism. Once independence was achieved, leaders realised that Slovenians needed to determine their identity and ask questions by using the arts as a medium. Government support is therefore high.

The two fields that remain relatively untapped are modern music and literature. Few musicians, bands or writers have reached any form of success outside national borders, with the exception of the poet France Prešeren – and his success dates back to the early 19th century.

Artistic work is rarely translated from its original Slovenian, which perhaps explains the relative obscurity of many of the country's most celebrated modern talents. The fact that the country is the third-smallest market for literature in Europe doesn't help matters much. In this country, selling 500 copies of a book will get you on the bestseller list.

Locally produced television and film aren't very successful either. As most residents speak English and the quality of Slovenian-produced television is so poor, there are few reasons to watch it. Independence may have provided Slovenia with a proud, new identity – but it has also limited the market to which artists can showcase their work. Success will only come with exposure, and further entrenchment into the European Union.

⬤ *Bird's-eye view of the city centre*

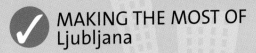

MAKING THE MOST OF
Ljubljana

Shopping

Despite the fact that Ljubljana is a European capital, shopping options may not at first glance seem all that spectacular. However, there are some great shops here – you just have to dig around a little. The Left Bank Centre's main shopping street, Slovenska (see page 78), contains a find for fans of both shopping and architecture; **Centromerkur** (ⓐ Trubarjeva cesta 1 ❶ (01) 426 3170), the city's oldest department store, is housed in a building of real art nouveau refinement.

The best place for everyday shopping is the **BTC City Shopping Centre** (ⓐ Smartinska 152 ❶ (01) 585 1100 Ⓦ www.btc-city.com), which is housed in a rather unprepossessing edifice just out of town. This provides a collection of high street stores, while the Emporium, a building that's actually inside the BTC complex, contains some of the more designer-style clothing chains – looking good is a serious consideration here, and people are prepared to pay. Visitors considering coming to Ljubljana primarily for a shopping-filled short break may want to think twice about scheduling for a weekend. Most shops in the centre close firmly at 13.00 on Saturday afternoons and don't even think about reopening until Monday morning.

Other shopping possibilities lie tucked away in the side streets of the Left Bank Centre (see page 70) and Old Town (see page 60), which provide a mixed bag of tourist traps and local designer boutiques. Local design work tends to be stylish, sleek and affordable when compared with similar products in Paris and London. The best bet for items of originality can be found every day in the stalls of the Central Market (see page 67).

Slovenian souvenirs are available in shops all over Ljubljana; however, most items associated with Slovenia are actually produced regionally, outside of the city. If you are planning an extensive tour of the country, save your purchases of arts and crafts until you visit the region in which the items are famous. Purchases to consider include fine lace, bottles of brandy and wine, black pottery, glassware, beehive panels and honey.

Antiques, especially from the art nouveau period, are great purchases in the city. There are a number of boutiques that specialise in the period – all featuring well-maintained and/or restored items for fans of this genre. Shipping is easy to arrange and can often be negotiated at very advantageous rates.

USEFUL SHOPPING PHRASES

What time do the shops open/close?
Ob kateri uri se zaprejo/odprejo trgovine?
Ob kateree ooree seh zapreyo/od-preh-yoh trhgoveeneh?

How much is this?
Koliko stane tole?
Koleeko staneh toleh?

Can I try this on?
Lahko tole pomerim?
Lakhko toleh pomereem?

My size is ...
Nosim številko ...
Noseem shteveelko ...

I'll take this one, thank you
Tega bi vzel(a), prosim
Tega bee oozel(a) prosseem

This is too large/too small/too expensive. Do you have any others?
Tole je preveliko/premajhno/predrago. Imate še kaj drugega?
Toleh yeh preveleeko/premaykhno/predrago. Eemateh sheh kay droogega?

Eating & drinking

When it comes to cuisine, Slovenia is influenced by all four bordering countries. Hungarian-style goulash, Viener schnitzel, grilled Balkan meats and Italian pizza and pasta are all widely available. Judging by the number of pizzerias in Slovenia, it could be argued that Italy actually stole this favourite menu item from Slovenians.

Traditional restaurants remain popular and usually fall into two categories: tourist-oriented eateries featuring Slovenian *gostilna*-style architecture and servers clad in local costume, or hole-in-the-wall establishments with hearty patrons and even heartier (and heavier) dishes. In either case, the meal is sure to be lip-smackingly good.

The country doesn't have a large immigrant population – and therefore doesn't have a wealth of cuisines it can offer visitors. Recent imports are beginning to make inroads into the Ljubljana dining scene, but quality tends to vary (along with the authenticity of the dishes). These include a wave of Mexican and Chinese

● *Take time out for a coffee or a horse-meat sandwich*

PRICE CATEGORIES
The restaurant price guides indicate the approximate cost of a three-course meal for one person, excluding drinks, at the time of writing.
£ up to €10   ££ €10–20   £££ over €20

establishments and more recently Japanese, Indian and Thai restaurants. Outside Ljubljana, you will be mainly restricted to Slovenian establishments and pizzerias.

Vegetarians beware! Always check with the establishment to see if a dish is truly meat-free. In many cases, locals will, intriguingly, think that chicken and ham don't count as meat.

Every meal in Slovenia will be accompanied by bread. On a gluten-free diet? You'll have to break it during your stay – especially when faced with the variety of doughy treats on offer. Specialities include wholewheat bread and 'mottled' bread made from three different types of dough (buckwheat, wheat and corn). For a real treat, be sure to try the braided Christmas loaves available throughout the city during the run-up to the holiday.

Another filling Slovenian option is groats. Made from barley, buckwheat or corn, these dense 'porridges' are often served with a savoury side dish such as pork crackling – definitely not for those looking to lose weight.

No meal is complete for a Slovenian unless it includes meat. The most commonly served are veal, beef, game and, above all, pork. Chicken and goose are rarely dished up. Also popular are fish and shellfish, even in mountainous regions. Trout caught in the Soča River is especially valued.

Before the main course is presented, diners often start with a bowl of soup. This is usually made from chicken or beef broth with an added dash of small egg noodles. In winter, soups can be much thicker and include potatoes, beans, smoked pork, sausage or sauerkraut. These traditional potages were designed as a filling, warm dish to help alleviate hunger and banish the cold during the long winter months.

Locals can often be found snacking on Slovenian dessert delicacies. The most common choice is potica, a kind of nut roll eaten during the day with coffee or tea, although other varieties filled with poppy seeds, walnuts, sultanas and apples are also popular.

Find yourself stuck for a snack? You won't be for long, considering the sheer number of food stands dotted throughout the city. The two most common are *burek*, which is a kind of flaky pastry filled with cheese or mince, and 'horse-meat sandwiches', which are exactly what they sound like – large sandwiches filled with horse meat.

When it comes to the constant fight against dehydration, be sure to try Slovenian wine. The country has been making wine since the days of the Roman Empire – and most of the best varieties never even leave the country. Many visitors think that the best wine comes from the Primorska region, which is famous for producing strong, fiery reds. Others prefer the dry, light reds found in the region of Posavje, which runs across the Sava River from eastern Štajerska. All of Slovenia's 14 wine regions boast an official wine route – so if you have a particular interest, be sure to inquire about maps and trails at the tourist information centre of the region you are hoping to visit.

Other drinks worth trying out are locally produced beers, ciders and a sort of honeyed brandy served straight from the fridge during the summer months.

USEFUL DINING PHRASES

I would like a table for ... people
Rad(a) bi mizo za ...
Rad(a) bee meezo za ...

May I have the bill, please?
Račun, prosim?
Rachoon prosseem?

Could I have it well-cooked/medium/rare, please?
Rad(a) bi dobro/pečen zrezek/zrezek po angleško?
Rad(a) bee dobro/pechen zrezek/zrezek po angleshko?

I am a vegetarian. Does this contain meat?
Vegetarijanec sem/Vegetarijanka sem. (fem.) Ali ta jed
vsebuje meso?
Veh-geh-tar-yahnets sehm/Veh-geh-tar-yahn-kah sehm.
Ah-lee tah yed vseh-boo-yeh meh-saw?

Where is the toilet (restroom) please?
Oprostite, kje je stranišče (toaleta)?
Oprossteeteh, kyeh yeh straneeshcheh (toaleta)?

I would like a cup of/two cups of/another coffee/tea
Kavo/čaj, prosim. Dve kavi/dva čaja, prosim. Še eno kavo/
še en čaj, prosim
Kavo/chay prosseem. Dve kavee/dva chaya, prosseem.
Sheh eno kavo/sheh en chay, prosseem

Entertainment & nightlife

When it comes to life after dark, Ljubljana as yet poses no threat to Las Vegas. While a blossoming alternative scene is beginning to emerge and the effect of a dedication towards design is taking shape, the city's population just isn't large enough to support a diverse scene.

Ljubljana's youth tends to dictate the types of activities a visitor might find there. The former squats and barracks of Metelkova (see page 82) and the converted prison at the Hostel Celica (see pages 18 & 37) attract a bohemian crowd. This is the place to go if you like your clubs rough, ready, adventurous and welcoming. Designer labels certainly aren't de rigueur.

The Left Bank Centre area (see page 70) hosts a wide range of high-end, well-respected cultural institutions including the Slovenian National Drama Theatre (see page 83). While performances do draw a well-bred crowd, they certainly aren't as stuffy as productions in nearby Austria or Italy. They still shouldn't be a place to debut your new trainers, however. What might be pennies for you is a fortune for most locals. Many will have saved up long and hard for a ticket.

Closer to the river is where the city's best cafés and restaurants can be found. Knafijev Prehod is a pedestrianised street upon which many atmospheric bars and eateries can be found. On warm nights, these venues positively heave with both locals and visitors. Many will offer outdoor tables so you can make the most of the weather and enjoy Slovenia's favourite pastime – people-watching.

Summer is a time of festivals and Slovenians always love a good performance, especially when it's free. At various times throughout the season, Prešernov trg is transformed into a free performance venue, complete with live musicians and dance. You may not have heard of any of the players, but all the world will be a stage when you join the masses as they dance and sing along with the performers.

🔺 *Street entertainment is free for all*

As Krakovo and Trnovo (see page 84) are very residential, bars and clubs in this district are extremely welcoming. You'll invariably be greeted warmly at any of the venues in these neighbourhoods, making them great regions to explore if you're visiting Ljubljana on your own. These neighbourhoods remain the district of choice for artists, students and squatters due to the proximity to **Ljubljana University** (ⓐ Kongresni trg). Students also bring a bit of a late-night vibe to the area, making it one of the only neighbourhoods (other than the area around the bus station) where you are guaranteed to find a bite of *burek* throughout the evening.

The bar scene, thanks to votes of confidence from a number of style bibles, is starting to heat up. Most of the newest venues have a 'less is more' mentality, preferring minimalism and modernism when designing interiors. These drinking dens are great if you want to surround yourself with a stylish crowd, but aren't that great if you're looking to meet locals as patrons usually keep to their individual groups.

Clubbers don't really have much of a choice in Ljubljana, but the venues are generally quite crowded providing a great party atmosphere. Aside from the previously mentioned Metelkova complex (see page 82), the most popular location for a night of dancing is the Bacchus Centre Club (see page 81). These multi-level, multi-venue centres of pleasure offer everything from techno to rock. Don't expect anything that sways too far from a Eurotrash beat.

The further you travel from the city centre, the less you will find that pubs, bars and clubs (and, for that matter, restaurants) work to set opening times: it's always best to phone and check times beforehand if you've got your heart set on visiting a particular venue.

◀ *Night time along the banks of the Ljubljanica River*

Sport & relaxation

SPECTATOR SPORTS

It really isn't the Slovenian way to spectate when they could be up and at it themselves. As evidence of this, the local football team, NK Olimpija, ceased playing in 2005, due to general lack of interest.

PARTICIPATION SPORTS

Keeping fit Fitness centres are dotted throughout the city, though most locals prefer to keep fit by incorporating exercise into their daily lives, rather than sweat in an airless room. However, if you're keen to pursue a prescribed fitness routine while you're here, most hotels of at least 3-star quality will offer basic facilities, including cardio and weight machines. Among the many good gyms is:

Tivoli Recreation Centre Fitness centre with an indoor swimming pool, tennis courts, roller-skating rink, ice rink and sauna.
ⓐ Celovška cesta 25 ⓣ (01) 431 5155 ⓛ 09.00–21.00

Tivoli Park (see page 92) was built for the local populace in the early 19th century. In the summer, the massive green space positively buzzes with activity. At all hours of the day, you will spot joggers, picnickers, families, Frisbee throwers and office workers basking in the sun. As the park is so large (or at least large for Ljubljana at 5 sq km, or 2 sq miles), it is perfectly possible to wander off the paths into hidden, tree-covered corners that feel like something straight out of a fairy tale.

RELAXATION

Gentle activity is also performed in the form of walking and promenading. During the summer a relaxing stroll up and down the banks of the Ljubljanica River is considered the height of fashion. Most will traverse the stretch between the Dragon and Cobbler's Bridge. Adventurous souls can, however, continue on until they reach the Trnovo Bridge before they turn back to the city centre.

● Tivoli Park

Accommodation

Slovenia's status as a chic city-break destination is a bonus for travellers. Unfortunately, there is still something of a dearth of quality city-centre hotels and prices remain high. If you don't book in advance you could find yourself out of luck in your search for a hotel room – both during the week and on weekends.

Those who like their hotels with a bit more character won't be disappointed. Renovations, restorations and rebuilds have created new properties, including antique-packed salutes to art nouveau, sleek and chic boutique properties, and *grande dame* hotels featuring restored interiors. The city outskirts, while inconvenient geographically, offer some great bargains for fans of modern minimalism, while the streets around Prešernov trg feature 4- and 5-star historic hotels. Finally, for those on a budget, Ljubljana's hostels are an excellent choice. Not only are prices reasonable, they are probably the most well-maintained and most character-filled dorm rooms and beds in Europe. One of them is even in a former army prison!

HOTELS

Hotel Emonec £–££ A reasonably priced hotel that's centrally located. It may not be the prettiest of buildings, but the rooms

PRICE CATEGORIES

Hotels in Slovenia are graded according to a voluntary star system, running from 1 star for a cheap guesthouse to 5 stars for a luxurious property with numerous facilities. All prices are for two people for a single night in a double room.

£ up to €80 **££** €80–140 **£££** over €140

are well decorated and the Emonec boasts a facility that you don't find everywhere – an electric massage chair! Who needs pretty?
ⓐ Wolfova ulica 12, off Prešernov trg ⓣ (01) 200 1520
ⓦ www.hotel-emonec.com

Park Hotel £–££ A budget hotel that's always a good option. While the hotel is located in an uninviting concrete tower, rooms are comfortable (if a little basic). ⓐ Tabor 9 ⓣ (01) 300 2500
ⓦ www.hotelpark.si

City Hotel Turist ££ Quality 3-star hotel designed for business travellers. Rooms are en suite and air-conditioned. On-street parking and cycle hire are available. Comfortable, secure, though lacking any real character. ⓐ Dalmatinova 15, off Prešernov trg ⓣ (01) 239 0000

Hotel Ljubljana ££ Hi-tech and not a little glam. Rooms feature massive plasma-screen TVs, virtual sightseeing tours of the city and broadband internet access. Other facilities include an indoor pool, saunas, gym and full-scale casino. While it's located 3 km (2 miles) from the city centre, a regular hotel shuttle bus is available to take guests to and from Prešernov trg. ⓐ Dunajska 160 ⓣ (01) 569 1192
ⓦ www.austria-trent.si

Antiq Hotel ££–£££ This boutique hotel has a great location, just under the castle and in the Old Town centre; all rooms have a different style. There is one budget room, and it's always in demand. ⓐ Gornji trg 3 ⓣ (01) 421 3560 ⓦ www.antiqhotel.si

Grand Hotel Union Business ££–£££ This modern hotel is a wing of the historic Grand Hotel Union Executive located next door (see page 37). While the exterior isn't as inspiring as its more famous neighbour, the interiors are almost exactly the same and guests can use all the original's facilities. ➋ Miklošičeva 3 ☏ (01) 308 1170 ⓦ www.gh-union.si

Grand Hotel Union Garni ££–£££ Centrally located, this modern hotel is convenient and comfortable. While the Business should be your first choice (see above), the Garni is a nice second option. ➋ Miklošičeva 9 ☏ (01) 308 4300 ⓦ www.gh-union.si

⬣ *The Grand Hotel Union Executive is one of the finest hotels in town*

Slon Best Western Premier ££–£££ Shoppers rejoice at the location of this great hotel in the middle of Slovenska. ❸ Slovenska 34 ❶ (01) 470 1100 Ⓦ www.hotelslon.com

Grand Hotel Union Executive £££ Beautiful art nouveau *grande dame* hotel considered to be the finest in town. It's convenient for the entire city. Rooms are classically designed (if a little uninspired). Higher floors provide the best views. ❸ Miklošičeva 1 ❶ (01) 308 1270 Ⓦ www.gh-union.si

Lev Hotel £££ This modern hotel is the city's only 5-star property. Designed with the business traveller in mind, it lacks a little in luxury considering the price. Rooms are spacious, if a bit bland – but the facilities are top-notch. ❸ Vošnjakova 1, off Celovška cesta ❶ (01) 433 2155 Ⓦ www.hotel-lev.si

GUESTHOUSES
Pension Pri Mraku £–££ This old-world guesthouse is designed with a bohemian feel, complete with old-fashioned draperies made from luxurious fabrics. ❸ Rimska 4 ❶ (01) 421 9600 Ⓦ www.daj-dam.si

HOSTELS
Alibi Hostel £ Slap bang in the middle of the Old Town and overlooking the Ljubljanica, this friendly, hundred-bed hostel has no curfew and the considerable distinctions of being very friendly and great for children. Cycle hire is available. ❸ Cankarjevo nabrezje 27 ❶ (01) 251 1244 Ⓦ www.alibi.si

Celica Hostel £ A converted military barracks that's one of the hottest places to stay in town. Constantly fully booked, the Celica offers rooms of 2, 3, 4, 5, 7 and 14 beds. Each room has been designed by a different local artist, with results varying from austere simplicity to overwhelmingly colourful. Smaller rooms require you to share bathroom facilities, while rooms for four or more people offer en suite toilets and showers. There is a room for disabled guests on the ground floor. At night, the place is hopping with hip 20- and 30-somethings drawn by the Arabic-inspired bar, tasty restaurant and cheap internet access.

If you need your sleep, Celica may not be the place for you. The floors echo, so even a simple whisper can sound deafening. ⓐ Metelkova 8 ⓣ (01) 230 9700 ⓦ www.souhostel.com

Ljubljana Youth Hostel £ Even though this is 3 km (nearly 2 miles) out of town – bus numbers 5 and 9 will get you into the city centre very quickly – it's definitely worth considering as its facilities are well above the norm and you get a 50 per cent discount on the use of sports equipment. ⓐ Litijska 57 ⓣ (01) 548 0055 ⓔ info@yh-ljubljana.com

Vila Veselova £ Located in a lovely old (as in 'charming', not as in 'derelict') building, this hostel has everything you'd expect, plus parking and air conditioning. It also places a priority on providing an atmosphere that's conducive to chilling out. ⓐ Veselova 14, off Tivolska cesta ⓣ (059) 926 721 ⓦ www.v-v.si

◗ *Popular Celica Hostel has individually designed rooms*

THE BEST OF LJUBLJANA

Ljubljana is ideal for a short break, because it's easy to get around. Explore the Old City for history, the Left Bank for culture, Krakovo and Trnovo for community, or Tivoli for outdoor pursuits. For daytrip suggestions, see pages 42–3.

TOP 10 ATTRACTIONS

- **Ljubljana Castle** This hilltop castle provides breathtaking views over the city as far as the Julian Alps. Don't miss the multimedia movie shown at the base of the tower (see page 64)

- **Prešernov trg** Ljubljana's main square always buzzes with activity. Approach it from the Triple Bridge to enjoy the best in local architecture (see page 72)

- **Ljubljanica River** The river is Ljubljana's heart. During summer months, the banks are packed with couples, friends, families and visitors. Pull up a chair at one of the cafés and watch the world pass by (see page 44)

- **Tivoli** Get away from the hustle and bustle of city life in Ljubljana's urban park paradise (see page 92)

- **Celica Hostel** Local bohemians hang out at this restored and renovated army building. A great place to mix with the local in-crowd (see pages 18 & 37)

- **Central Market** Stalls and shops run by local farmers and artisans, selling crafts and fresh produce (see page 67)

- **Križanke** Explore this cultural centre that was once home to a large monastery (see page 83)

- **Slovenska** Time for shopping! Great boutiques and designer goodies await you on this main artery (see page 78)

- **Narodni Muzej Slovenije (National Museum of Slovenia)** Slovenia's largest and most extensive museum holds a treasure-trove of artefacts (see page 76)

- **Bled** Just an hour outside of town is Ljubljana's favourite rural retreat. Go for a day or a week – there's plenty to see, do and enjoy (see page 102)

⬇ *Aerial view of the city*

Suggested itineraries

HALF-DAY: LJUBLJANA IN A HURRY

It's easy to see the bulk of the city's biggest sites in just a few hours. Start your day at Ljubljana Castle (see page 64) by taking the train from Prešernov trg. Trains leave hourly, so check the schedule before planning your day. A one-minute funicular is another option leaving from Krekov trg. Explore the castle grounds, being sure not to miss going up the tower, and then follow Študentovska as it snakes down to Vodnikov trg. From here, it's just steps away to the Central Market (see page 67), with its wares and goodies, ending up at Dragon Bridge, just north of the tourist information centre (see page 153).

1 DAY: TIME TO SEE A LITTLE MORE

Follow the itinerary outlined above and continue your explorations of the Old Town by following the river along the riverside path. Pass the Triple Bridge (on your right) and the river will begin to bend to the left. Enjoy the walk along the road, also known as Cankarjevo Nabrežje, being sure to veer away from the river to enjoy the small, character-filled side streets.

2–3 DAYS: TIME TO SEE MUCH MORE

With two or three days you can get a much better impression of what the city has to offer. Take the recommended tour for day one. Follow this with explorations of Tivoli Park (see page 92), including cycling along the various park paths. On day three, choose a walk around the museums in the far west of the neighbourhood known as Centre. Alternatively, head down to Krakovo and Trnovo (see page 84) to visit these creative communities.

LONGER: ENJOYING LJUBLJANA TO THE FULL

Get more out of Ljubljana by getting out of town. A visit to Bled (see page 102) will afford you lakeside splendour, while Piran (see page 120) is a jewel of a seaside destination. Both places will provide memories that you will treasure.

⬤ *Lake Bled is a popular trip from the capital*

Something for nothing

Some of Slovenia's best sights are absolutely free. Locals aren't rich and they have mastered the art of having a good time for very little money. One of the most treasured experiences is a simple stroll along the banks of the Ljubljanica River. While the cafés will do their best to help part you from your money, there is no need to sit down at one of the tables. Instead, just walk along the riverfront as far as the Trnovo Bridge (see page 86). In fact, the bridges of Ljubljana are some of the most treasured sights in the city, particularly the graceful sweep of the Triple Bridge (see page 64) designed by Jože Plečnik (see page 86). For just a few cents more, you can even splurge on a delicious cone of *gelato* (ice cream).

Speaking of Plečnik, architecture is one of the main draws of the Slovenian capital. The city is packed with art nouveau treasures and there are plenty of opportunities to see these beautiful examples of design, particularly along Miklošičeva Cesta (see page 72).

Another cheap and cheerful option is a walk through Tivoli (see page 92). This large park is a popular place for a picnic or kickabout with friends. Bikes can be rented for very little if you want to enjoy the network of paths. Alternatively, just explore the various fields and hills.

Many of Ljubljana's smaller museums are free of charge, including the Brewery Museum (see page 97), the DESSA Architectural Gallery (see page 75), the **Tobacco Museum** (ⓐ Tobačna 5 ⓣ (01) 477 7344) and the **Slovenian School Museum** (ⓐ Plečnikov trg 1 ⓣ (01) 251 3024). While the collections aren't as filled with the 'wow' factor as some of the other galleries in the city, they all exhibit wonderful slices of Slovenian life you might not find elsewhere.

Finally, if you want to see the big sights and save money, consider purchasing the Ljubljana Card at the Tourist Information Centre, or on-line (via www.ljubljana-tourism.si). This discount card provides money off admission fees, cafés, club entrance charges, hotel accommodation, restaurant meals and shops for a period of 72 hours. Free bus transportation is also included in the price of the card, which costs €12.52.

⬤ *The city's abundant art nouveau architecture is free for all to enjoy*

When it rains

Ljubljana can be a bit of a challenge when the weather turns, but it's a challenge you can meet. One of the best things to do if the clouds look a little grey is to head for the museums located in and around Prešernova in the west end of Centre. The collections on display at the **Museum of Modern Art** (ⓐ Tomšičeva 14 ⓣ (01) 241 6800), the National Gallery (see page 75) and the National Museum of Slovenia (see page 76) are extensive enough to warrant hours, if not a full day, of exploration – a perfect option to help pass a rainy day.

Another possibility – and one that children will probably find more interesting – is to head out of town to the Postojna Caves (see page 124). By bus or train, the caves are about one hour away from Ljubljana, and offer plenty of fascinating opportunities for both kids and adults. Visitors book themselves onto tours that take them 1,700 m (5,577 ft) into the cave system by train before walking along a prescribed route past the Big Mountain, along the Russian Bridge and into the Concert Hall. Along the way, you will see fantastic stalagmites, stalactites, curtains of rock formation and columns. Just before reaching the concert hall, there is a small tank filled with four examples of the legendary 'human fish' or, of course, *Proteus anguinus*. Sometimes mistaken by locals for baby dragons, this blind salamander is native to the cave system and can breathe both in and out of water.

Finally, if you want to shop till you drop, then the best option is to take a taxi out to the BTC City shopping centre (see page 22). While this centre offers a wide selection of shops, the actual walkways between each shop aren't covered – so it's a good idea to wear a coat. If unique wares are what you're looking for, then don't bother planning a visit. With few exceptions, most of the brands are the usual high-street names that you'll be used to back home.

◆ *The Postojna Caves are great for exploring*

On arrival

TIME DIFFERENCE

Slovenian clocks follow Central European Time (CET). During Daylight Saving Time (end Mar–end Oct), the clocks are put ahead by one hour.

ARRIVING

By air

Most visitors will arrive by plane at Ljubljana's **Jože Pučnik Airport**, commonly known as **Brnik Airport** (ⓐ Brnik 130a ⓣ (04) 206 1000 ⓦ www.lju-airport.si), which is 27 km (17 miles) from the city centre. Other airports are available at **Portorož** (ⓦ www.portoroz-airport.si) and **Maribor** (ⓦ www.maribor-airport.si), but these tend only to be used by the smaller, regional carriers, although in 2007 **Ryanair** (ⓦ www. ryanair.com) began flying from Maribor to London. Though Brnik Airport has all of the usual services, such as duty-free shopping, a bureaux de change and café, it does sometimes feel like you're landing in a farmer's field. However, since 2006 renovations have been underway, and in 2007 a new passenger terminal was opened. The image of Ljubljana Airport is changing as the modernising and upgrading continues.

A taxi will take approximately 30–45 minutes to reach the city centre, depending on traffic, and cost in the region of €40. Frequent bus services provide the most affordable option for airport transfer. However, this service is drastically reduced on weekends, so check schedules in advance. By bus, you will reach Ljubljana in about 40 minutes, depending on the number of stops and traffic. The cost of a one-way ticket is between €3.50 and €5, depending on which company you use. Buses leave the airport every hour on the hour from 05.00–20.00 Mon–Fri, or at 07.00 and then every two hours

⬥ *Mestni trg's towering Robbov Fountain*

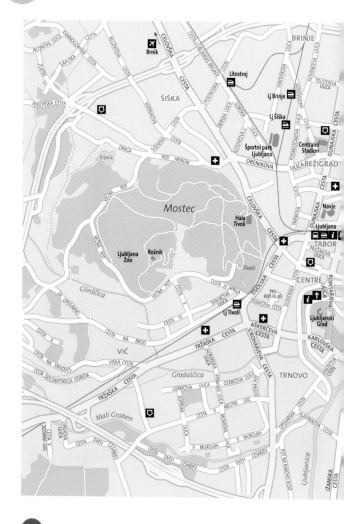

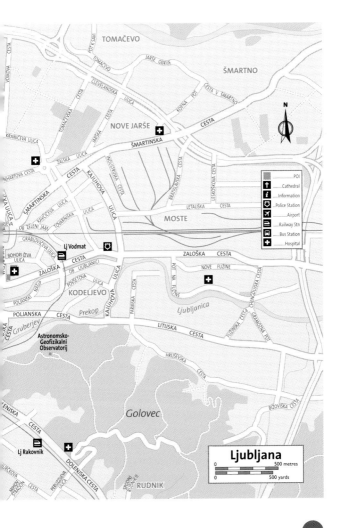

Ljubljana

	POI
✝	Cathedral
ℹ	Information
	Police Station
✈	Airport
	Railway Stn
	Bus Station
✚	Hospital

0 ——— 500 metres
0 ——— 500 yards

between 10.00 and 20.00 on weekends and holidays. From the city centre, it's the same schedule, but buses leave at ten past the hour instead of on the hour. The journey time is 45 minutes. **Markun** (📞 (041) 792 865 🌐 www.prevozi-markun.com) offers a private bus service between the airport and **Ljubljana Bus Station** (📍 Trg osvobodilne fronte 4), which departs from the airport daily at 05:45, 06:40, 10.55, 12.40, 14.30, 16.00, 17.30, 18.25, 22.55 and 00.00. Buses for the airport leave Ljubljana at 05.20, 06.15, 10.25, 12.15, 14.00, 15.30, 17.00 and 22.30. The times are adjusted to the exact times of the flights so it is advisable to reserve in advance. However, there is generally a bus waiting for every plane that lands. The journey time is 30 minutes and the fare is €5 to the bus station or €9 to any address in Ljubljana.

By rail

Ljubljana railway station (📍 Trg OF 6 📞 (01) 291 3332 🌐 www.slo-zeleznice.si) is not exactly the hub of an extensive rail system, but it can be reached from most parts of Europe. The main line used by locals is the one that runs between Ljubljana and Maribor, the second-largest city of Slovenia. This line also has spurs that branch off to Novo Mesto and Zagreb (Croatia) via Sevnica. Other lines include a north-south line that runs from the Croatian coast up to the Austrian border via Ljubljana, and another line that avoids the capital altogether, running close to the coast and into Italy.

By road

Slovenia is an easy country to drive in, unless you have a fear of heights. Mountainous roads are limited to single lanes and can wind precariously for hours. City streets are well marked and well lit, and the motorway system is fast – except on Friday and Sunday

IF YOU GET LOST, TRY ...

Excuse me, do you speak English?
Oprostite, ali govorite angleško?
Oprossteeteh, alee govoreeteh angleshko?

**Excuse me, is this the right way to ... the cathedral/
the tourist office/the old town?**
Oprostite, je to prava pot do ... Katedrale/
turističnega urada/starega mesta?
*Oprossteeteh, yeh to prava pot do ... katedraleh/
tooreesteechnega oorada/starega messta?*

Can you point to it on my map?
Mi lahko pokažete na karti mesta?
Mee lakhko pokazheteh na kartee messta?

evenings – efficient and extensive. From the cities of Western Europe,
drive either to Trieste in Italy, where you can go northeast by picking
up the E61/E70/A1 to Ljubljana, or cut down through Germany and
Austria and join the E61/A2 southeast to Ljubljana via Bled. From
here, it is relatively easy to get into the centre by following the signs.
Parking is available both on-street and in protected lots. You may
even qualify for free parking at your hotel. Consider selecting a more
expensive property that includes parking in the room cost, if you plan
on bringing your car.

The city's bus station (see page 52) has a steady stream of services
to and from all major Slovenian cities.

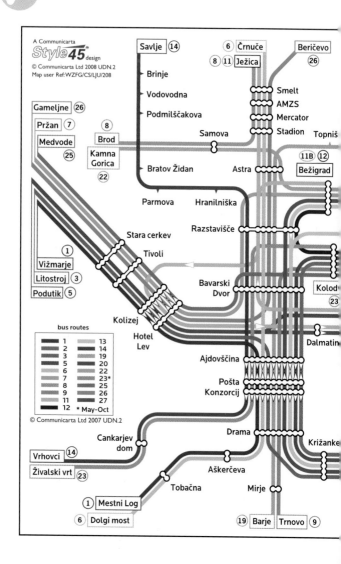

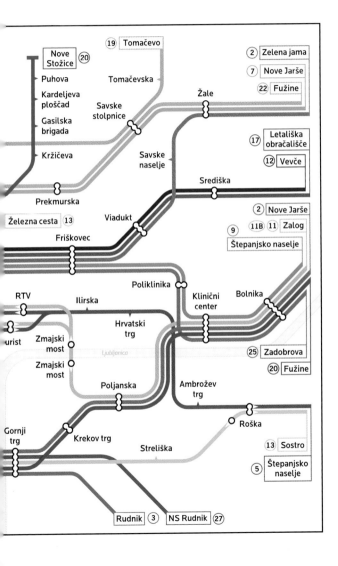

FINDING YOUR FEET

Ljubljana is a small city of individual neighbourhoods. When exploring specific districts, walking is easily the best option. However, a well-maintained network of buses is available. For travel between districts, taxis can be used but they're expensive – and on weekends they're very hard to find.

ORIENTATION

The Slovenian capital is a compact city, with the Ljubljanica River cutting right through the centre. The Old Town (see page 60) is situated on the right bank and is made up of short, thin streets that were designed to accommodate little more than horse traffic. This is the neighbourhood that can trace its history back the furthest. As such, roads in this neighbourhood can get quite clogged, due to their modest size.

Ljubljana Castle (see page 64) lies on a hill overlooking this part of town and can be reached using various staircases or winding roads. To save time or energy, take the funicular from Krekov trg or board one of the regular trains that depart from Stritarjeva ulica throughout the day.

The Left Bank, opened up following the completion of bridges during the 17th century, offers wider streets and larger properties.

As you follow the Left Bank district westwards, it becomes the 'Centre' neighbourhood (see page 70) – a bustling community of government buildings and cultural institutions. While the architecture becomes less interesting in this part of town, the volume of museums grows, especially on the aptly named Muzejska ulica.

Furthest to the west is Tivoli Park, a 5-sq-km (2-sq-mile) swathe of greenery that is well used and well loved by residents. During the day, joggers, cyclists and skateboarders all congregate on the numerous paths, while office workers set up picnics during their lunch hours. Sights in this part of town are few, but the natural beauty more than makes up for the lack of landmarks.

The residential neighbourhoods of Krakovo and Trnovo (see page 84) lie to the south. Visit this region if you want to experience a slice of Slovenian life. Artists, students and bohemians call this district home, and the result is a colourful collection of cafés, street scenes and nightspots that are well worth an evening or two of your time.

● *Playing on the steps of the Town Hall*

GETTING AROUND

Ljubljana is an extremely easy city to get around. While there is a system of buses and trains, you probably won't ever need to use these, as the city centre is so tiny. From Prešernov trg, it's possible to get anywhere in town (including the farthest reaches of Tivoli) in about 15–20 minutes at a brisk walking pace. If you are feeling a little lazy, there are over 20 bus routes to choose from, running approximately every 15 minutes from 05.00–22.30 and a few night buses (running between 03.15–05.00). Single journeys can be paid for on board and cost a flat rate of €1. If you plan on making several journeys, pick up tokens (*žetoni*) for €0.80 at the post office or news-stands. For a map of the bus system, see pages 54–5.

A word of caution if you decide to take a train anywhere in Slovenia: stations named after a prominent town are often actually located many kilometres from your desired destination.

CAR HIRE

If you are planning to make just one or two small trips in Slovenia, for example to Bled (see page 102), then public transport is most convenient. However, if you would like to see a lot of the country and explore it in more depth then hiring a car is definitely recommended. Although public transport is available it takes a lot longer than it would by car and can end up being quite expensive if there are many of you. Please note, some of the mountainous roads can be quite treacherous, so if you have a fear of heights you may want to avoid driving altogether.

Rates vary according to season and length of hire, but there are many special offers available – check the internet. The minimum age for renting a car varies between 18 and 21.

◗ *View from Triple Bridge to the Italianate Franciscan Church*

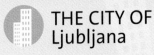

Old Town

Ljubljana's Old Town is the ancient heart of the city. Winding streets, cobbled passages and a stunning hilltop castle provide plenty of atmosphere that is tailor-made for romance and intrigue. For the best views over Ljubljana and beyond, head straight to the top of the Castle Belvedere tower (see page 65).

The Old Town is where you will find the best shopping, most historic buildings and secret architectural finds. Pick up a few goodies at the Central Market (see page 67) before getting lost in the maze-like streets. Only by wandering the Old Town's courtyards and lanes will you truly be able to savour everything that this ancient neighbourhood has to offer.

SIGHTS & ATTRACTIONS

Botanični Vrt (Botanical Garden)

Situated 800 m (2,625 ft) southeast of Old Town proper, this small collection of flora was founded in 1810 and contains approximately 4,500 species of plants, trees and flowers, of which about one-third are native to Slovenia. ⓐ Ižanska cesta 15 ⓣ (01) 427 1280 ⓛ 07.00–19.00 Apr–June, Sept & Oct; 07.00–20.00 July & Aug; 07.00–17.00 Nov–Mar

Cathedral

It may not have an original name, but Ljubljana's cathedral boasts a long and proud history. A church has existed in this location since the 13th century, but the present structure only harks back to the early 1700s. While the interiors aren't to everyone's taste – all baroque gilt, pink marble, stucco and frescoes – the choir stalls are spectacular. The two bronze doors at the main entrance are a recent addition,

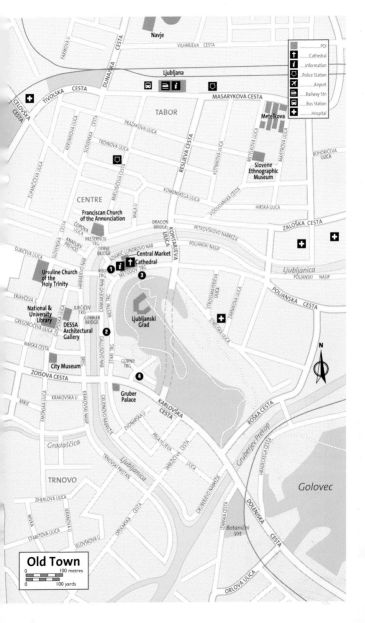

introduced to celebrate the visit of Pope John Paul II in 1996.
🅐 Dolničarjeva ulica 1 ☎ (01) 234 2697 🕐 10.00—12.00, 15.00—18.00

Cobbler Bridge

Many consider the bridges of Ljubljana to be the most famous sights
in the city – and for good reason. Cobbler Bridge, when originally
built, was intended as a centre for trade and it created a lot of
revenue for the feudal lords through the tolls collected from all
who used it to pass in and out of the Old City.

Dragon Bridge

This bridge is the last of the four famous bridges to cross the
Ljubljanica, yet is also one of its most graceful. Built in the early
20th century, the bridge is topped by dragons. There is an old legend
that says the dragons will wag their tales each time a virgin passes.
Now's your chance.

Gornji trg (Gornji Square)

This extension of Stari trg is notable for its collection of medieval
houses and the Church of St Florian – a place of worship built in
1672 after a devastating fire that destroyed much of the old town.
The church is dedicated to the patron saint of fires.

Mestni trg (Town Square)

This is the most important square in the Old Town and would have
been the focal point of all activity during the Middle Ages. Today the
name is given to a more extensive area of side streets. Overlooking
proceedings is the town hall, which remains the seat of city
government – a role it has performed since it was built in the late
15th century. Inside is a Gothic courtyard with an arcade that once

hosted theatrical performances. Lying on top of the building is the symbol of Ljubljana, a golden dragon.

Stari trg (Old Square)

Stari trg is the traditional heart of the Old Town. Here is where the shops of yesteryear would have battled it out for the wallets of Ljubljana's medieval residents. The houses that line the square today are reconstructions from the 19th century, but a few of the original buildings can be spotted if you take a quick jaunt down the adjoining cobbled passageways and into the serene courtyards.

⬥ *The dragon is a traditional symbol for the city*

Triple Bridge

Leading from Prešernov trg to Old Town, the Triple Bridge is the main span that crosses the Ljubljanica River and also one of the most admired. Designed by the architect Jože Plečnik in 1943 (see page 86), the bridge is essentially a combination of the original Špital Bridge with two (almost) parallel spans to form a – you guessed it – triple bridge. In terms of foot traffic, it remains the most-used bridge in the city.

CULTURE

Gruber Palace

This palace, which now holds the collections of the national archives, was the original home of Gabriel Gruber. A prominent Jesuit, Gruber was responsible for building the canal that regulates the Ljubljanica River. The palace is a rare example of the Zopf style (see page 13).

From the main entrance, look east along the Karlovška Cesta where you will see what remains of the city's old Balkan Gate.
ⓐ Zvezdarska ulica 1 ⓑ Visit by appointment only, which must be arranged in person

Ljubljanski Grad (Ljubljana Castle)

Ljubljana Castle, built in the 16th century, dominates the skyline as it stands imperiously on the top of Castle Hill. Considered the most important spot in the city, due to its location on top of the region's highest point, the castle was a royal residence through much of the 17th and 18th centuries.

As the castle fell out of favour architecturally, its strong walls and fortifications proved excellent assets for the national barracks and prison until well into the 20th century.

🔺 *Ljubljana's castle dominates the city's skyline*

Today, the bulk of the castle has been renovated to its original splendour and most traces of the prison have been erased.

Try to include a visit to the Belvedere. This tower, located on the western side of the castle courtyard, provides stunning views over the entire city and beyond to the Alps. The extra expense is certainly worth the investment. Also of interest is a stop at the Virtual Museum, a 20-minute 3-D movie that takes visitors on a quick tour through Ljubljana's most influential periods.

While climbing up the Belvedere Tower, give yourself a few minutes to peak inside the Chapel of Saint George. Built in 1489, this fresco-covered place of worship features many depictions of the coats of arms of Ljubljana's ruling families.

⬥ *A guided tour of the city, on wheels*

Guided tours of the castle, museum, tower and grounds are available during the summer months at 10.00 and 16.00. Join the group on the bridge located at the castle's main entrance. Also, if the prospect of climbing up Castle Hill to see Ljubljanski Grad doesn't appeal, take advantage of the convenient tourist train that leaves from Prešernov trg every hour on the hour between 09.00 and 18.00. Alternatively, take the funicular which connects the Ljubljana Castle with the old city core. It operates every ten minutes between 09.00–23.00 May–Sept & 10.00–21.00 Oct–Apr. ⓐ Ljubljanski Grad ⓦ www.festival-lj.si ⓛ 09.00–22.00 May–Sept; 10.00–21.00 Oct–Apr; Belvedere Tower: 09.00–21.00 May–Sept; 10.00–18.00 Oct–Apr

RETAIL THERAPY

The Old Town is a shopper's paradise, especially if you like quirky shops in atmospheric streets and alleys.

OLD TOWN MARKETS

There is simply no better place to barter and binge than Ljubljana's Central Market. Lying just across the Triple Bridge from Prešernov trg, this open-air marketplace sells fresh fruit, cheeses and souvenirs all week long. Another seasonal market that's well worth a look is the Sunday-morning antiques market held in Pogačarjev trg. You'll want to be browsing by at least 8am to stand any chance of picking up a real bargain, but there are always lots of items you won't find anywhere else.

Other markets worth browsing through are the **Antiques Flea Market** (ⓐ Cankarjevo nabrežje), held every Sunday from 08.00–14.00, and the arts and crafts stalls that open every working day near the Cathedral (see page 60), under the colonnade. In summer there is also a weekly art market of paintings and ceramics every Saturday between May and September from 09.00–16.00.

Cajna Hisa A small shop with tea and porcelain that makes great gifts for friends and family at home. Attached to the shop is a cosy tea café. ⓐ Stari trg 3 ⓣ (01) 421 2444 ⓛ 10.00–19.00 Mon–Fri, 10.00–18.30 Sat, closed Sun

Dom Excellent carved wooden *objets d'art* and locally produced pottery are just some of the speciality items found at this pleasant home furnishings store. ⓐ Mestni trg 24 ⓣ (01) 241 8300 ⓛ 09.00–19.00 Mon–Fri, 10.00–15.00 Sat, closed Sun

Piranske soline For those who prefer a local original souvenir: the shop offers a varied selection of items connected to salt. ⓐ Mestni trg 19 ⓣ (01) 425 0190 ⓦ www.soline.si ⓛ 09.30–19.00 Mon–Fri, 10.00–15.00 Sat & Sun

Rustika A great souvenir shop and art gallery located inside Ljubljana Castle. ⓐ Ljubljanski Grad, Grajska planota 1 ⓣ (01) 383 3247 ⓛ 10.00–19.00 Oct–May; 09.30–20.00 June–Sept

Vale Novak The shop has several floors, with Slovenian and English books, designer clothing and a small bar. ⓐ Tavcarjeva ulica 5, off Slovenska cesta ⓣ (01) 230 9572 ⓛ 09.00–19.00 Mon–Fri, 09.00–13.00 Sat & Sun

TAKING A BREAK

Abecedarium Café £ ❶ Once the residence of a famous Slovenian writer, this house (the oldest in Ljubljana, dating back to 1528) is now a delightful teahouse that serves up coffees, pastries and many more treats. ⓐ Ribji trg 2 ⓣ (01) 426 9514 ⓛ 07.00–01.00

AFTER DARK

RESTAURANTS
Café Romeo £–££ ❷ Trendy café-restaurant along the Ljubljanica River. The pancakes are renowned. ⓐ Stari trg 6 ⓣ (01) 426 9011 ⓛ 10.00–01.00

Sokol £–££ ❸ While the interiors are far from authentic, the food certainly is. Everyone pops into this faux-rustic eatery to nosh on local nibbles or grab a cup of coffee. ⓐ Metodov trg 18 ⓣ (01) 439 6855 ⓛ 06.00–23.00

Spajza ££–£££ ❹ Meat, fish, vegetarian – all is on the menu. The restaurant has several rooms; if you are with a bigger group and would like some privacy in a quaint setting, this is the place. In the summer they also open their courtyard with outdoor tables. ⓐ Gornji trg 28 ⓣ (01) 425 3094 ⓛ 12.00–23.00 Mon–Sat, 12.00–22.00 Sun

BARS, CLUBS & DISCOS

Café Galerija If you feel like some relaxation, the café (which is actually a club) has an exotic feel to it and provides couches for a nice lie down. ⓐ Mestni trg 5 ⓣ (01) 426 0327 ⓦ www.gpa.si/galerija ⓛ 19.00–23.30 Mon–Fri, 20.00–01.00 Sat, 20.00–22.00 Sun

Hvala za roze The location of this bar makes it unique: it's in the cellars of the former fish market. ⓐ Adamic-Lundrovo nabrezje 5 ⓛ 08.00–04.00 Mon–Sat, 08.00–02.30 Sun

Maček This bar-café on the right bank of the Ljubljanica is the place to see and be seen. ⓐ Krojaška ulica 5, off Hribarjevo nab ⓣ (01) 425 3791 ⓛ 08.30–00.30

Movia Vinoteka Drink your way through the wines of Slovenia at this well-stocked wine bar. Regular wine tastings that highlight local vintages are programmed. ⓐ Mestni trg 2 ⓣ (01) 425 5448 ⓛ 15.00–00.00 Mon–Fri, 12.00–00.00 Sat, 12.00–22.00 Sun

Pr'Skelet As the name of the bar might suggest, the décor is skeletal (and some bits even move). ⓐ Kljucavnicarska ulica 5, off Hribarjevo nab ⓣ (01) 252 7799 ⓛ 17.00–00.00 Mon–Fri, 12.00–01.00 Sat, 12.00–23.00 Sun

Left Bank Centre

Ljubljana's Left Bank is the place where locals do their business, meet up with friends, are entertained and savour culture. Here is where you'll find the best galleries and museums, the most attractive bars, and the finest examples of art nouveau construction (see page 12). The Left Bank grew in popularity as the Old Town began to grow outside the ancient city walls. Aristocrats were drawn to the larger plots of land and greater privacy afforded by the neighbourhoods across the river and they moved in droves. Today's chic and elite continue to flock to the Left Bank – this time in search of the perfect riverside table to enjoy drinks and dinner with friends. On summer evenings, the cafés alongside the Ljubljanica River swarm with activity.

SIGHTS & ATTRACTIONS

Franciscan Church of the Annunciation

From the exterior, this church looks like it should have some promising treasures lying within. Unfortunately, with the exception of a glass coffin holding the rather gruesome remains of a saint by the name of Deodatus, there is little to warrant a trip inside this 17th-century Italianate structure. ⓐ Prešernov trg 4 ⓣ (01) 425 3007 ⓛ 06.45–12.30, 15.00–20.00

Kongresni trg (Congress Square)

Ljubljana hosted the Congress of the Holy Alliance between Austria, Russia, Naples and Prussia in 1821, and this is the square named to honour the event. In the centre of the square is a park known as Zvezda (meaning 'star'), due to the shape in which the trees are planted. You may find yourself surrounded by students at all hours

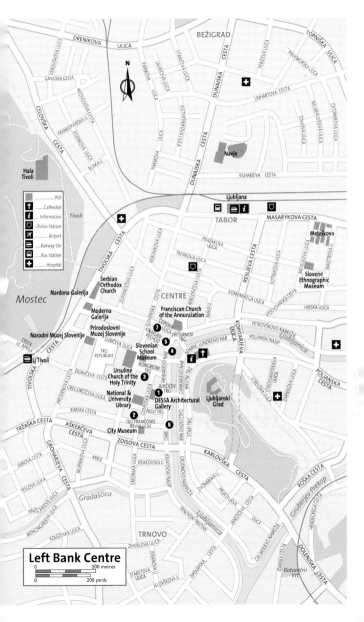

Left Bank Centre

0		200 metres		
0		200 yards		

Map labels:

DRENIKOVA ULICA

BEŽIGRAD

TOPNIŠKA ULICA

GASILSKA CESTA

VEROVŠKOVA ULICA

SYNNOVA CESTA

PREKMURSKA ULICA

PERCEVA ULICA

MEDVEDOVA CESTA

FRANKOPANSKA CESTA

ČRNOVA ULICA

RUSKA ULICA

PARMOVA

LAPREJOVA ULICA

DUNAJSKA CESTA

PETTENKOFOVA ULICA

LINHARTOVA CESTA

NEUBERGERJEVA ULICA

CHTOMOROVA ULICA

STIHOVA ULICA

CELOVŠKA CESTA

Hala Tivoli

Tivoli

PARMOVA ULICA

DUNAJSKA CESTA

Navje

VILHARJEVA CESTA

Ljubljana

MASARYKOVA CESTA

TABOR

Metelkova

PRAŽAKOVA ULICA

REŠLJEVA CESTA

KOTNIKOVA ULICA

METELKOVA ULICA

MASTROVA ULICA

Slovene Ethnographic Museum

TIVOLSKA CESTA

KERSNIKOVA ULICA

TRDINOVA ULICA

Serbian Orthodox Church

ŽUPANČIČEVA ULICA

CENTRE

KOMENSKEGA ULICA

HIRSKA ULICA

Nardona Galerija

Mostec

Moderna Galerija

Prirodoslovni Muzej Slovenije

Narodni Muzej Slovenije

Franciscan Church of the Annunciation

PREŠERNOV TRG

SLOVENSKA CESTA

TOPOVA ULICA

ČOPOVA ULICA

MIKLOŠIČEVA CESTA

PETKOVŠKOVO NABREŽJE

POLJANSKI NASIP

KOMITARJEVA

Ljubljanica

⑦

NAZORJEVA ULICA

PLEHNOVA

⑤

Slovenian School Museum

CANKARJEVO NAB

DALMATINOVO NAB

STROSSMAYERJEVA

④

HRIBARJEVO NAB

Hospital

CESTA 27. APRILA

SUBIČEVA ULICA

KONGRESNI TRG

③

MESTNI TRG

Ljubljanski Grad

POLJANSKA CESTA

TRG REPUBLIKE

 Li Tivoli

ERJAVČEVA ULICA

Ursuline Church of the Holy Trinity

KRIŽEVNIŠKA ULICA

ZARNIKOVA ULICA

TIVOLSKA CESTA

GREGORČIČEVA ULICA

GOSPOSKA ULICA

①

DESSA Architectural Gallery

PREŠERNOVA CESTA

National & University Library

⑥

STARI TRG

Grubeljev Prekop

RIMSKA CESTA

TRG FRANCOSKE REVOLUCIJE

②

NOVI TRG

BREG

GALLUSOVO NABREŽJE

TRŽAŠKA CESTA

AŠKERČEVA CESTA

City Museum

ZOISOVA CESTA

KARLOVŠKA CESTA

ROŠKA CESTA

JAMOVA CESTA

GROHARJEVA CESTA

MURNIKOVA ULICA

MIRJE

EMONSKA ULICA

KRAKOVSKA U.

KRIŽEVA ULICA

BARJANSKA CESTA

TVONSKA ULICA

PRIJATELJEVA ULICA

TESLOVA ULICA

FINŽGARJEVA ULICA

MENCINGERJEVA ULICA

KOLEZIJSKA ULICA

Gradaščica

Ljubljanica

HRADECKEGA CESTA

DOLENSKA CESTA

TRNOVO

ŽIHERLOVA ULICA

TRNOVSKI PRISTAN

JERANOVA U.

ILOVSKOVA U.

STARETOVA ULICA

JELOVŠKOVA U.

OPEKARSKA CESTA

GRUDNOVO NABREŽJE

JANŠEVA ULICA

OPEKARSKA CESTA

CRNUHARJEVO NABREŽJE

JANSKA ULICA

IŽANSKA CESTA

Botanični Vrt

N

Legend:

POI

Cathedral

Information

Police Station

Airport

Railway Stn

Bus Station

Hospital

of the day, due to the placement of Ljubljana University in a former ducal palace on the square's southern edge.

Miklošičeva Cesta

This main road links Prešernov trg with the train and bus stations, and is an art nouveau fan's paradise (see page 12).

Novi trg (New Square)

This meeting point south of the Cobbler's Bridge was originally situated outside the city walls in the Middle Ages. Fishermen called the area home until the 16th century, when aristocrats, charmed by the houses, decided to move in and gentrify the properties. Though many of the homes were destroyed during an earthquake in 1895, the square continues to be of interest due to the remains of the medieval Jewish quarter on Židovska ulica. The synagogue and much of the Jewish population are now gone, but the area retains a lot of its character. The **Slovenian Academy of Arts and Sciences** (Ⓦ www.savba.sk) is situated on the square's western end, and occasionally hosts intriguing exhibitions.

Prešernov trg (Prešernov Square)

Dedicated to the great Slovenian poet, this central square acts as the main artery linking the Left Bank with the Old Town. Considered the heart of the city, it is often used in summer for free concerts on warm evenings. Note the fine art nouveau architecture in the surrounding streets, and the statue erected in 1905, depicting Prešeren himself. Look closely at the plinth to see depictions and motifs of his most famous poems.

▶ *Prešeren, the famous Slovenian poet*

Serbian Orthodox Church

Every inch of this church's wall and ceiling-space is covered with modern frescoes. Dedicated to Saints Cyril and Methodius, it was built in 1936 and remains a popular place of worship for the local Serbian community. ⓐ Prešernova cesta ⓣ (01) 252 4002 ⓛ 14.00–18.00 Tues–Sun, closed Mon

Trg Republike (Republic Square)

The district's main square is also its most disappointing. Home to the Slovenian Parliament building, this concrete-strewn example of brutal communist architecture from the late 1950s (see page 12) is an uninspiring mess.

Ursuline Church of the Holy Trinity

Probably the most beautiful example of baroque architecture in the city, this church was built in 1726 and contains a spectacular African marble altar of many colours. To reach the church, go along the Plečnik underpass at the western end of Kongresni trg. As you approach the entrance, look to the right to see a golden statue resting at the top of a column. This statue is a copy of the fourth-century *Citizen of Emona*. The original is currently in the National Museum (see page 76). ⓐ Slovenska cesta 21 ⓣ (01) 252 4864 ⓛ 09.00–10.30, 16.30–19.00

CULTURE

City Museum

This small museum houses a collection of Roman artefacts that were discovered in and around the city, and a scale model of the ancient city of Emona, upon which Ljubljana now rests. ⓐ Gosposka ulica 15 ⓣ (01) 241 2500 ⓦ www.mm-lj.si ⓛ 10.00–18.00

🔺 *Typical architecture on the riverbank*

DESSA Architectural Gallery

This small gallery focuses on the work of the nation's finest contemporary architects. 🅐 Židovska steza 4, off Jurčičev trg
ⓘ (01) 251 6010 🕙 10.00–15.00

Narodna Galerija (National Gallery)

For an introduction to Slovenian art, head directly to this extensive gallery of portraits and landscapes. Works include medieval frescoes,

Gothic statues, and beautiful pieces from the hands of the national romantics (Künl, Karinger and Pernhart) and impressionists (Šubic and Jakopič). For pieces from outside Slovenia, including items from the Middle Ages and modern day, visit the modern north wing, which also houses temporary exhibitions and visiting artists. ➌ Prešernova ulica 24, off Tivolska cesta ➊ (01) 241 5434 Ⓦ www.ng-slo.si ➌ 10.00–18.00 Tues–Sun, closed Mon

Narodni Muzej Slovenije (National Museum of Slovenia)

This museum, considered by most to be the finest in the country, boasts a strong coin collection, and sections devoted to applied arts and history. While the Roman artefacts are pretty standard, the Vače situla Celtic pail unearthed east of Ljubljana is a highlight. ➌ Muzejska ulica 1 ➊ (01) 241 4400 Ⓦ www.narmuz-lj.si ➌ 10.00–18.00 Fri–Wed, 10.00–20.00 Thur

National & University Library

Considered to be architect Jože Plečnik's finest work (see page 86), this building was completed in 1941 and contains a breath-taking collection of books and historical documents. ➌ Gosposka ulica 14 ➊ (01) 200 1100 Ⓦ www.nuk.si ➌ 09.00–20.00 Mon–Fri, 09.00–14.00 Sat, closed Sun

Prirodoslovni Muzej Slovenije (Slovenian Museum of Natural History)

Sharing the same building as the National Museum (above), this collection of natural artefacts contains examples of reconstructed mammoth skeletons, stuffed birds, mammals and reptiles. Of particular interest are the mineral exhibits compiled by

⬤ *Look carefully for the detail carved on state buildings*

a 19th-century Baron and a display examining the unique salamander found in the Postojna Caves, *Proteus anguinus* (otherwise known as the 'human fish'). ⓐ Muzejska ulica 1 ① (01) 241 0940 ⓛ 10.00–18.00 Fri–Wed, 10.00–20.00 Thur

Slovene Ethnographic Museum

Slovenia's main museum on Slovenian, European and non-European collections of material, social and spiritual heritage items. It represents the traditional culture in Slovenia with the heritage of everyday (festive) life, knowledge, values, skills, wisdom and creativity in the Slovene ethnic sphere. ⓐ Metelkova ulica 2 ① (01) 300 8700 ⓦ www.etno-muzej.si ⓛ 10.00–18.00 Tues–Sun. Admission charge (except last Sun of each month)

RETAIL THERAPY

In shopping terms, everything revolves around the major street of Slovenska. If you can't saddle yourself with a frightening amount of credit card debt here, you are simply not putting in enough effort – all the opportunities await. Go on, get your limit increased.

Almira Sadar This leading Slovenian designer concocts amazing garments using materials that are 100 per cent natural. ⓐ Tavčarjeva ulica 6, off Slovenska cesta ① (01) 430 1329 ⓛ 09.00–19.00 Mon–Fri, 09.00–13.00 Sat, closed Sun

Antikvitete Novak Antiques, both authentic and reproduction. ⓐ Kongresni trg 1 ① (01) 426 6541 ⓛ 10.00–13.00, 16.00–19.00 Mon–Fri, 10.00–13.00 Sat, closed Sun

Vinoteka & Café Galerija Maximal Breg 2 For those who like a bit of art while they drink their wine, then enjoy a good Slovenian wine at this combination art gallery/wine bar. ⓐ Breg 2 ⓣ (01) 422 0033 ⓛ 09.00–01.00 Mon–Sat, closed Sun

TAKING A BREAK

Paninoteka £ ❶ If you're about to embark for Ljubljana Castle and you need a bite before you head to the top of the hill, drop by this small bar (there's no phone), where they have a rich choice of sandwiches, *tramezzini*, and freshly made salads. ⓐ Jurčičev trg 3 ⓛ 08.00–01.00 Mon–Sat, 09.00–23.00 Sun

Le Petit Café £ ❷ This café has a bohemian feel to it. Ideal for a croissant and a meet up with friends. ⓐ Trg francoske revolucije 4 ⓣ (01) 251 2575 ⓛ 07.30–23.00 Mon–Fri, 09.00–23.00 Sat & Sun

Zvezda £ ❸ If you like your coffee or tea with a pie, cupcake or some ice cream, Zvezda has it all on offer. The portions are rich; for those who prefer something smaller, there is one dinky pie called Mini Sadna Tortica – a little cupcake filled with cream and topped with strawberries. ⓐ Kongresni trg 4 ⓣ (01) 421 9090 ⓛ 08.00–21.00 Mon–Fri, 08.00–23.00 Sat, 08.00–18.00 Sun

AFTER DARK

RESTAURANTS
Makalonca £ ❹ This romantic outside café is as close as you can get to the Ljubljanica River flowing through the middle of the town

● *Enjoy a cocktail at the popular Cantina Mexicana*

centre. It's self-service. ❷ Hribarjevo nabrezje 19 🕐 10.00–00.00 Mon–Sat, 10.00–15.00 Sun, summer, closed winter

Cantina Mexicana £–££ ❺ Mexican food in Slovenia? Oh, it works. While the food is good, the location and interiors provide the special touch that makes this place a great locale for a leisurely meal. ❷ Knafljev prehod 3 ❶ (01) 426 9325 🕐 09.00–01.00

Namaste £–££ ❻ Namaste is, of course, Hindi for 'hello'. As well as chicken, lamb and seafood dishes, there are also many Northern Indian vegetarian specialities on the menu. ❷ Breg 8 ❶ (01) 425 0159 🕐 10.00–00.00 Mon–Fri, 11.00–00.00 Sat, 11.00–22.00 Sun ⓦ www.restavracija-namaste.si

Gostlina As ££–£££ ❼ Delicious seafood tailor-made for special occasions. The wine list is particularly well chosen. ❷ Čopova ulica 5a ❶ (01) 425 8822 🕐 12.00–03.00

BARS, CLUBS & DISCOS

Bacchus Centre Club This clubbing centre has a restaurant, lounge-bar and large dance floor, so you're bound to find something you like. Probably the most popular place in town. ❷ Kongresni trg 3 ❶ (01) 241 8243 🕐 20.00–05.00 Tues–Sat, closed Sun & Mon

Dvorni Bar A classy joint that offers many wines, among which are some of the finest of Slovenia. Keep an eye on their website for wine-tastings. ❷ Dvorni trg 2, off Prešernov trg ❶ (01) 251 1257 ⓦ www.dvornibar.net 🕐 20.00–00.00

SQUARES, TAKE COVER – THIS IS METELKOVA

Lurking in Left Bank Centre, in the rather unassuming – and that's putting it generously – location of a former Fourth of July barracks, is the city's entire alternative scene. Inspired by the squatters of Copenhagen's Christiania, a group of locals occupied the building (there was no-one in) and transformed it into Metelkova, almost certainly Slovenia's leading 'Autonomous Culture Zone'. This is a hot-bed of on-the-edge activity: a number of clubs call it home, including a hardcore punk venue (Channel Zero) and a mainstream centre for international DJs (Klub Gromka). Opening times change frequently (depending on when the organisers' mums say they've got to be in), so do check the website. ⓐ Between Metelkova ulica & Maistrova ulica ⓦ www.metelkova.org

CINEMAS & THEATRES

Café Teater For modern comedies, musicals and popular entertainment, book tickets at Café Teater, which is located in the Knights Hall of the Križanke arts complex (see page 83). ⓐ Trg francoske revolucije 1–2 ⓣ (01) 252 7108 ⓦ www.cafe-teater.si

Cankanjev Dom The main venue for concerts and performances is this cultural centre named in honour of the novelist and playwright Ivan Cankar. Two large auditoriums and a dozen smaller performance spaces designed for acoustic sets and chamber music host over a thousand cultural events each year. Acoustics in the Gallus Hall are said to be superb. ⓐ Prešernova cesta 10 ⓣ (01) 241 7100 ⓦ www.cd-cc.si

Križanke Home to the Ljubljana Summer Festival (see page 10), this arts complex has had a long and varied history. The Teutonic Knights of the Cross built this as their command centre in the 13th century and it acted as a focal point for city power until 1714, when it was transformed into a monastery. Today, it houses an open-air theatre with seating for 1,400 people. Look immediately in front of the complex for the Ilirija Column, dedicated to Napoleon. Slovenians greatly admired and respected Napoleon because he made Ljubljana his regional capital and allowed Slovenian to be taught in school for the first time in the country's history. ❷ Trg francoske revolucije 1–2 ❶ (01) 241 6000

Opera House Built in 1892, and originally named the 'Provincial Theatre', this theatre once programmed a season of German and Slovene productions. Today, it houses the Slovenian National Opera and Ballet companies, and performances are in Slovene only. ❷ Župančičeva ulica 1 ❶ (01) 241 1740 ❿ www.balet.si

Philharmonic Hall The Slovenian Philharmonic Orchestra was founded in 1701 and is now one of the oldest in the world to be in continuous operation. Honorary members have included Beethoven, Brahms and Haydn, while Gustav Mahler was resident conductor during the season of 1881–82. ❸ Kongresni trg 10 ❶ (01) 241 0800

Slovenian National Drama Theatre An art nouveau treat (see page 12) that's the home of Slovenia's national theatre company. Performances are in Slovenian only. ❷ Erjavčeva cesta 1 ❶ (01) 252 1511 ❿ www.drama.si

Krakovo & Trnovo

The two neighbourhoods of Krakovo and Trnovo are often ignored by tourists, who usually favour the more obvious sights of the city centre. To do this is to miss Ljubljana's residential heart. These two districts, located to the south of the Old Town, offer a number of interesting buildings – many built by the area's local hero, architect Jože Plečnik (see page 86).

Once considered Ljubljana's Montmartre, due to the number of artists who called its streets home, Krakovo and Trnovo still have a strong artistic flavour. To experience 'La Vie Boheme', head down to the bars along the Ljubljanica near the Trnovo Bridge. The people-watching possibilities in warm weather are top-notch.

SIGHTS & ATTRACTIONS

Church of St John the Baptist

Originally built in 1855, this church is neo-Romanesque in design, yet remains extremely bare inside. With the exception of the ceiling frescoes by artist Matej Sternen, there is very little to warrant a stop. Fans of the work of Prešeren should note that it was inside this church that the poet first saw the love of his life, Julija Primic. Unfortunately for him, she only wanted to be friends.
③ Kolezijska ulica 1 ① (01) 283 5060 ① 18.00–20.00 Mon–Sat, 08.00–12.00 Sun

Jakopič Garden

Famed Slovenian impressionist Rihard Jakopič worked extensively in this 'garden'. Also the site of some Roman ruins, it is still possible to see the black and white mosaics and remains of a complex

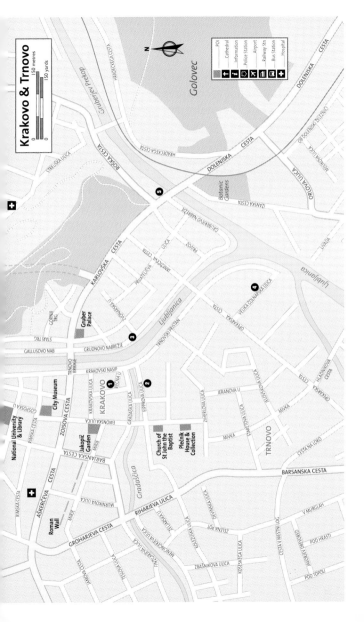

PLEČNIK HOUSE & COLLECTION
(LJUBLJANA ARCHITECTURAL MUSEUM)

Jože Plečnik lived in this house from 1921 until his death in 1957. Considered one of Slovenia's finest sons, he was in many ways the superstar of the former-Yugoslavian architectural scene (see page 12), in that he managed to synthesise existing forms and turn them into something new. Plečnik was responsible for the bulk of the city's most highly regarded buildings and bridges. This collection perfectly preserves his books, equipment, furniture and notes almost exactly as they were found at the time of his death. One of the quirkier items is a chair in the kitchen that was specially designed to allow Plečnik to eat and work at the same time. ❸ Karunova ulica 4, near Ziherlova ulica ❶ (01) 280 1600 ⓦ www.aml.si ⏰ 10.00–15.00 Mon & Fri, 10.00–18.00 Tue, Wed & Thur, 09.00–15.00 Sat, closed Sun

heating system. It is only possible to view the artefacts from the gate – so if Roman history is of great interest to you, make an appointment before you arrive. ❸ Mirje 4 ❶ (01) 241 2506 ⏰ by appointment only

Trnovo Bridge

Plečnik (see above) designed and built this bridge in 1932. Considered one of the three great bridges of Ljubljana (along with the Triple Bridge and Dragon Bridge), this is the one few tourists see due to its distance from the city centre. What makes this bridge so notable is its collection of five pyramids – a Plečnik trademark – that lie alongside it.

⬤ *The original Roman wall that used to surround the city*

RETAIL THERAPY

While Krakovo and Trnovo may be residential districts, they aren't all that popular when it comes to shopping. Due to Ljubljana's compact size, residents still prefer to make the short trek into the Old Town to spend their money. Thus, the options here aren't exactly overwhelming. Convenience stores, supermarkets and uninspiring clothing tend to constitute the bulk of what's on offer. Keep your wallet in your pocket and save your cash for the boutiques in the city centre.

Annapurna Shop If you're considering a trek into the Julian Alps but have forgotten your sleeping bag, then kit yourself out here. Almost anything you might need for all-season explorations is available. ⓐ Krakovski nasip 4 ⓣ (01) 426 3428 ⓦ www.annapurna.si ⓛ 09.00–19.00 Mon–Fri, 09.00–13.00 Sat, closed Sun

TAKING A BREAK

For a delightful rest after a day exploring the neighbourhood, look for Eipprova ulica – a leafy street that runs east from the Trnovo Bridge along the southern embankment of Gradaščica. This collection of cafés and bars is colourful and quirky, appealing to the district's artistic and outspoken residents. Choose any of the eateries for a good meal surrounded by friendly local folk.

AFTER DARK

RESTAURANTS & CAFÉS
Pri Škofju £ ❶ Especially popular for weekend breakfasts, this tasty restaurant in the heart of Krakovo is considered by many to offer

⬣ *The marina is a great place to relax*

⬤ *Residential areas are filled with character*

the best Slovenian dishes in town. ⓐ Rečna ulica 8 ⓣ (01) 426 4508
🕒 10.00–00.00 Mon–Fri, 12.00–00.00 Sat & Sun

Sax Pub £ ❷ A great place for a pint and a platter of Slovenian nibbles.
Live jazz is offered every Thursday evening at 22.00. ⓐ Eipprova
ulica 7 ⓣ (01) 283 9009 🕒 10.00–01.00 Tues–Sun, closed Mon

Trta £ ❸ Known as the best pizzeria among locals because of its use of fresh ingredients. ⓐ Grudnovo nabrezje 21 ❶ (01) 426 5066 ⓦ www.trta.si ❶ 11.00–22.30 Mon–Fri, 12.00–22.30 Sat, closed Sun

Pri Jerneju £–££ ❹ Cosy and comfortable *gostilne* (inn) serving solid takes on Slovenian favourites. Definitely one of the better options if you're looking to try local cuisine. ⓐ Velika Čolnarska ulica 17 ❶ (01) 283 8735 ❶ 12.00–23.00 Mon–Sat, 12.00–19.00 Sun

Yildiz Han ££ ❺ It can sometimes feel a bit kitsch, what with all the belly dancing and live Turkish music, but if you're with a group then this Turkish eatery is a lot of fun. Run by a friendly family, it's a solid choice for a spicy, yet tasty, night on the town. ⓐ Karlovška cesta 19 ❶ (01) 426 5717 ❶ 11.00–00.00 Mon–Sat, closed Sun

BARS, CLUBS & DISCOS
Trnovski Zvon Pub When the Sax (see page 90) is packed, this studenty pub makes for a great second-choice venue. While it's not as hip, it's also not as crowded. Try to sit at one of the outdoor tables to enjoy the street traffic. ⓐ Eipprova ulica 17 ❶ (01) 283 9496 ❶ 09.00–23.00 Mon–Fri, 11.00–23.00 Sat, 12.00–22.00 Sun

CINEMAS & THEATRES
KUD France Prešeren Centre Dedicated to presenting 'non-traditional' artistic events, this society programmes an eclectic mix of literary events, spoken-word performances, workshops and exhibitions. Not for fans of Broadway musicals. ⓐ Karunova ulica 14 ❶ (01) 283 2288 ⓦ www.kud-fp.si ❶ 11.00–01.00 Mon–Sat, 15.00–01.00 Sun

Tivoli

Tivoli draws its name from the massive park situated at its centre. Considered the green lungs of the city, this 5-sq-km (2-sq-mile) area of parkland, which was designed in 1813, positively heaves on summer days, when locals who haven't got the time or money to head out to the coast or up into the mountains choose to while away their time on the area's grassy slopes. What makes this park special is the fact that this collection of paths, trees and meadows is probably loved more by its residents than New Yorkers love Central Park or Londoners love Hyde Park. Nature is adored by Slovenians – almost all of whom wish that they could afford a country retreat for those weekends when Ljubljana is packed with tourists. As soon as the sun comes out, locals will plan picnics and impromptu kick-about sessions of footie. If you want to join the active crowds, why not consider renting a bicycle at any of the numerous booths?

Whatever you do, don't litter or leave anything behind. Even stubbing out a cigarette is frowned upon. Mother Nature deserves respect and the locals won't be afraid to tell you this if they see you doing something that might harm her.

SIGHTS & ATTRACTIONS

Krajinski Park Tivoli

This main green artery of Ljubljana is loved by this city of rural worshippers. It's a popular spot for walking, biking, picnics and outdoor sports. On the southeastern edge of the park is Krajinski Park Tivoli – a series of walkways, fountains and benches that meander through the landscaped grasses. Children especially love

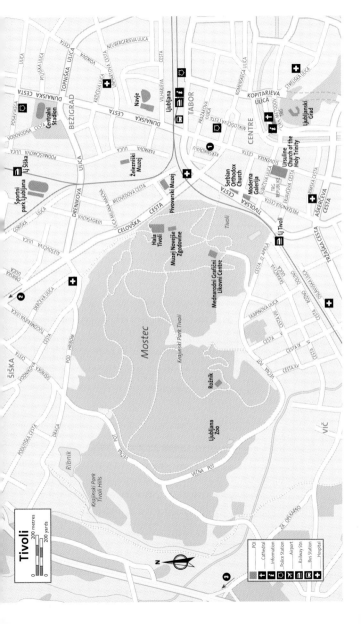

the lower level of this orderly park, drawn by the playground and recreation centre, complete with swimming pool, bowling alleys and tennis courts.

Krajinski Park Tivoli Hills
The bulk of the Park Tivoli is made up by a series of hills, of which Rožnik Hill is the most visited. Here is where travellers can find the church of St Mary and a number of countryside restaurants that feel like they should be situated in Bled, rather than minutes from the centre of Ljubljana. Active types especially love this section of the park, and can often be found walking, jogging or cycling along the paths.

Ljubljana Zoo
Over 500 animals representing 120 species are on display at this collection located on the southern slope of Rožnik Hill. The cages are a bit small and some of the visitors taunt the animals mercilessly – but children especially love the petting zoo. ⓐ Živalski Vrt Ljubljana ⓘ (01) 244 2188 Ⓦ www.zoo.si Ⓛ 09.00–19.00 May–Aug, 09.00–16.00 Sept–Apr

CULTURE

Mednarodni Grafični Likovni Centre (International Centre of Graphic Arts)
Housed in the 17th-century Tivoli mansion, this centre hosts the International Biennial of Graphic Arts (see page 10) during odd-numbered years. When not in use for this, temporary exhibitions

Ⓓ *The mansion in Tivoli Park*

are offered, changing every three months. ⓐ Pod turnom 3, off Večna pot ⓣ (01) 241 3818 ⓦ www.mglc-lj.si ⓛ 11.00–18.00 Wed–Sun, closed Mon & Tues

Muzej Novejše Zgodovine (Museum of Modern History)

Explore the history of Slovenia's last hundred years at this multimedia-heavy collection of exhibits chronicling the 20th century. Housed in an 18th-century mansion, the museum examines both the Communist era and the explosion of commercialism following the destruction of the Iron Curtain. ⓐ Celovška cesta 23 ⓣ (01) 300 9610 ⓦ www.muzej-nz.si ⓛ 10.00–18.00

Pivovarski Muzej (Brewery Museum)

Slovenia's favourite beer is Union, and this museum allows you to wander around the brewery to examine the magic of hops and yeast. Tours are only available to groups, but individuals can sometimes get inside if they call ahead to arrange a special visit. Unless you're really fascinated by beer, don't go out of your way to book. ⓐ Pivovarniska ulica 2 ⓣ (01) 471 7330 ⓛ 08.00–13.00 first Tues of each month, by appointment only

Železniški Muzej (Railway Museum)

This museum, spread over two sites, hosts a surprisingly large collection of locomotives from Slovenia's rail history. Everything from hulking engines to old-fashioned wagons is on offer, including items that date back to the early days of the country's network when the original rails were laid by the Austro-Hungarians. ⓐ Parmova 35 and Kurilniška 3 ⓣ (01) 291 2641 ⓛ 10.00–18.00 Tues–Sun, closed Mon

ⓞ *A show of strength: monument for the people*

TAKING A BREAK

Kava Caj £ ❶ A coffee and tearoom in a more tranquil part of the city. It looks small from the outside, but once you're in look for the stairs. There is another floor leading to an upper room and a courtyard which opens in summer. ⓐ Kersnikova ulica 1 ❶ (01) 433 8233

AFTER DARK

RESTAURANTS

Casa del Papa £–££ ❷ Dedicated to the memory of Ernest Hemingway, this restaurant serves up the dishes of the countries that most influenced him throughout his life: Spain, Cuba and America. Always popular, it's a great place if another meal of dumplings and meat just won't do. ⓐ Celovška cesta 54a ❶ (01) 434 3158 ❷ 12.00–01.00

Pod Rožnikom ££ ❸ Out of the way but well-loved by locals, this restaurant serves spicy Southern Slavic cuisine, including such mouth-watering items as *pljeskavica* (spicy meat patties) and *prebranac* (beans and onions slow-cooked in an earthernware pot). Veggie items are few and far between. Go only if you have a completely empty stomach, as portions can be huge. ⓐ Cesta na Rožnik 18, off za Opekarno ❶ (01) 251 3446 ❷ 10.00–23.00 Mon–Fri, 11.00–23.00 Sat & Sun

---

❷ *You can enjoy a balmy ambience at a riverfront eatery*

● *The park in Tivoli offers a range of activities*

BARS, CLUBS & DISCOS

Opera Bar Ljubljana's cosmopolitan bar, a place to pose, and none the worse for that. ⓐ Cankarjeva cesta 12, off Tivolska cesta ① (01) 421 0390 ⓛ 07.00–00.00 Mon–Wed, 07.00–02.00 Thur & Fri, 08.00–02.00 Sat, 10.00–18.00 Sun

Sub Sub Club Founded by a collection of local DJs, nights vary wildly according to who happens to spin that evening. However, a crowd of the artistic, challenging and downright scary is guaranteed. Leave flashy duds and full wallets at home if you want to blend in. ⓐ Celovška cesta 25 ① (01) 515 3575 ⓛ 10.00–05.00 Fri & Sat, closed Sun–Thur

● *View of boats in the marina*

Northwest Slovenia

In an area of generally beautiful scenery, Northwest Slovenia excels. This is largely due to the Julian Alps, which form an unforgettable backdrop. Thus the area is popular as a hiking destination. Tour operators have transformed this pocket of the country into a popular weekend break and outdoor-orientated getaway destination, drawn by its picturesque setting and proximity to natural wonders and sporting opportunities. The area's leading town is Bled (see below). Bohinj (see page 108) is the name given to the towns, villages, valleys and mountains that make up the region encompassing the Sava Bohinjka basin, southwest of Bled. At the heart of this location is Lake Bohinj, a body of water with strong magical connections to Slovenian folklore.

GETTING THERE

By rail
Trains leave Ljubljana train station every hour for Bled (as they do for Bohinj), and arrive at **Lesce Bled International Station** (see Ⓦ www.bled.si for details).

By road
Buses leave Ljubljana bus station every hour for both Bled and Bohinj.

BLED

With the exception of Ljubljana, the town of Bled probably receives more foreign visitors than any other in Slovenia. Located on the banks of Lake Bled, the town can get extremely crowded during the summer season, when almost the entire population of Ljubljana

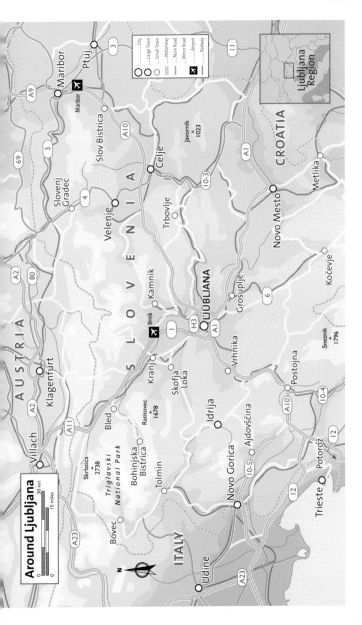

Around Ljubljana

	City
	Large Town
	Small Town
	Motorway
	Main Road
	Minor Road
	Railway
✈	Airport

Ljubljana Region

Striking decoration on a house in Bled

flocks to its cooler climes to escape the heat of the capital. Surrounded by soaring peaks, and offering views of the emerald-hued lake, church-dotted island and clifftop castle, the town offers many reasons to warrant a visit. Medieval pilgrims knew about the beauty of Bled for many years and transformed the area into a place of peace and prayer, most choosing to worship at the Church of the Assumption located on Bled Island in the middle of the lake.

SIGHTS & ATTRACTIONS

Bled Castle

Perched on the top of a rugged cliff, Bled Castle looks out over the lake and includes all the features most people associate with a typical medieval fort. Towers, moats, ramparts, ivy-covered walls, atmospheric cellars – all combine to create the perfect setting.

Built on two levels, the castle dates back to the 11th century, but most of what can be seen today was built in the 16th century. The southern wing houses a museum collection including coinage, armour, furniture and costume from various periods throughout the region's history. While many of the items were never actually used by the residents of the castle, they serve to give a good insight into how the Slovenian upper classes lived.

There is even an old-fashioned printing press where you can pick up prints of Bled lake scenes and a wine cellar staffed by a monk, selling bottles of local vintages. ❷ Grajska cesta 25 ❶ (04) 572 9780 ● 08.00–20.00 May–Oct, 08.00–17.00 Nov–Apr

BLED ISLAND

Site of a Christian church since the ninth century, this jewel of an island is a popular trip. Getting to the island is almost as much fun as exploring the island itself. Trips are made on regular gondolas that depart from Spa Park, the jetty below the tourist information centre and Milno on the south shore. If you're feeling active, you can also rent rowing boats. The main sight on the island is the baroque Church of the Assumption, which can be reached by following the South Staircase (built in 1655) past the Chaplain's House and Provost's House. Outside the church is a 15th-century belfry and wishing bell, which visitors ring if they want to ask for something special. ● 08.00–dusk

The enchanting island in Lake Bled

TAKING A BREAK

Slaščičarna Šmon £ Bled has a local pastry speciality in the form of the cream cake — essentially, it's a layer of vanilla custard combined with whipped cream and encased in two layers of flaky pastry. Very sweet. Very rich. And oh, so good. 🅐 Grajska cesta 3 🕔 (04) 574 1616 🕒 Variable, so phone to check

AFTER DARK

Restaurants

Mayer Penzion £–££ This Slovenian restaurant puts the focus on authenticity and uses only the finest local ingredients. Especially highly regarded for its selection of delicious Slovenian wines. 🅐 Želeška cesta 7 🕔 (04) 576 5740 🅦 www.mayer-sp.si 🕒 Variable, so phone to check

Restavracija Topolino £–££ A slow food inn where you can witness the culinary skills of the chef. Seasonal dishes. 🅐 Ljubljanska cesta 26 🕔 (04) 574 1781 🕒 12.00–23.00 Wed–Mon, closed Tues

Restavracija Okarina ££ This restaurant is probably the fanciest in town and dishes up traditional Slovenian options in a romantic setting. The interior may feel slightly kitsch, though. If it proves too much, try snaring a table on the back terrace. On weekends, the restaurant opens up its tandoori oven to add Indian meals to the menu. 🅐 Ljubljanska 8 🕔 (04) 574 1458 🕒 Variable, so phone to check

Bars, clubs & discos

Casino Bled The hottest nightspot in town. Roulette, baccarat, blackjack and slots are all on offer. Well suave. 🅐 Cesta Svoboda 15 🕔 (04) 574 1150 🅦 www.casino-bled.si 🕒 Constantly

Pub Bled Enjoy drinking and dancing to the wee hours in this friendly spot located opposite the Grand Hotel Toplice (see below). ⓐ Cesta Svobode 19a ⓣ (04) 574 2622 ⓛ Variable, so phone to check

ACCOMMODATION

Hotel Pension Pibernik £ Located on a clearing surrounded by the forest, in a tranquil setting. On one side of the buidling, all of the rooms have balconies. ⓐ Ljubljanska cesta 40 ⓣ (04) 574 1552

Alp Pension £–££ This pension is situated in a calm environment and offers comfortable rooms. There is a restaurant with local dishes. Other extras are the tennis court and the garden at the back of the pension. ⓐ Cankarjeva cesta 20a ⓣ (04) 574 1614 ⓦ www.alp-penzion.com

Grand Hotel Toplice ££–£££ Considered one of the finest hotels in the region, it can sometimes feel overrun by tour groups. Although some of the rooms can seem a tad gloomy, the views of the lake are superb. ⓐ Cesta Svobode 12 ⓣ (04) 579 1000 ⓦ www.hotel-toplice.com

BOHINJ

SIGHTS & ATTRACTIONS
Church of Saint John the Baptist

This small, medieval church is a real find. Filled with frescoes and located at the end of a stone bridge on a reflective lake, the church is a place of peace and beauty – perfect for a spot of quiet contemplation.

While the nave of the church is Romanesque, the presbytery is Gothic, dating from the mid-15th century. The most spectacular sections of the church are the presbytery's walls, arches and ceiling, which are covered with frescoes depicting biblical scenes. An interesting image to note is the picture of the three men singing above the angels with vampire teeth on the lower walls of the presbytery. These men have goitres, once a common problem for locals, due to the lack of iodine in their diet. ❸ Northern side of the Sava Bohinjka 🕐 09.00–12.00, 15.00–18.00 June–Sept, Oct–May by appointment only, the approach to be made in person

Savica Waterfall

This waterfall is a popular hiking destination, which provides beautiful backdrops as it carves into a gorge 60 m (197 ft) below. As the source of Slovenia's longest river, it's a well-known landmark, located along a well-marked footpath just 4 km (2½ miles) from the Hotel Zlatorog in Ukanc. The falls are most inspiring just after heavy rain. During such weather you will need to wear waterproof clothing in order to avoid getting soaked by the spray.

🔺 *Lake Bohinj with the Church of St John the Baptist*

CULTURE
Alpine Dairy Museum
This small collection located in Stara Fužina chronicles the history of dairy farming in the Bohinj valley. Until the late 1950s, this region of Slovenia was the most important producer of dairy foods in the nation, all by traditional methods. Displays in the museum include a mock-up of a 19th-century herder's cottage, old-fashioned presses and vats, and old photographs. ⓐ Stara fužina 181 ⓣ (04) 577 0156 ⓛ 10.00–12.00, 16.00–18.00 Tues–Sun, Jan–June, Sept & Oct; 11.00–19.00 Tues–Sun, July & Aug; closed Mon, Nov & Dec

Tomaž Godec Museum
Located in Bohinjska Bistrica, the main settlement of the Bohinj region, this museum chronicles the contributions of one of Slovenia's most noted communists. Godec was one of the founding members of the Slovene National Liberation Movement before being captured by the Germans during World War II. His life as a leather tanner, champion skier and mountaineer is examined in the exhibits on display. ⓐ Zoisova 15 ⓣ (04) 577 0142 ⓛ 10.00–12.00, 16.00–18.00 Wed, Sat & Sun, closed Mon & Tues, Thur & Fri, Jan–Apr; 10.00–12.00, 16.00–18.00 Tues–Sun, closed Mon, May, Sept & Oct; 10.00–12.00, 17.00–20.00 Tues–Sun, closed Mon, June–Aug

AFTER DARK
Restaurants
Gostlina Mihovc £ Popular with locals and visitors, this welcoming eatery dishes up thick soups, stews and goulash. Try not to get too drunk on the home-made brandy. ⓐ Stara fužina 118 ⓣ (04) 572 3390 ⓛ 10.00–00.00

Pizzerija Centre £ Toppings are pretty standard (no funky combinations here) but the central location makes up for the limited selection. As the only place to grab a bite in the centre of Ribčev laz, it can get crowded in season. ⓐ Ribčev Laz ⓣ (04) 572 3170 ⓛ Variable, so phone to check

Gostišče Rupa £–££ You'll need a car to reach this delightful tavern located in a village just below Studor Mountain. Dishes are of the home-cooked variety, featuring spectacularly fresh Bohinj trout, and dumplings made from buckwheat and cheese. Don't go if you aren't hungry. ⓐ Srednja vas 87 ⓣ (04) 572 3401 ⓛ 10.00–00.00 Tues–Sun, closed Mon

ACCOMMODATION

Planšar £ In such a rural location, why not stay in a farmhouse? This friendly place to rest your head is famous for its cheeses and has a comfortable apartment on-site, which can accommodate groups of up to seven people. ⓐ Stara fužina 179 ⓣ (04) 572 3095

Penzion Stare £–££ If you want to experience nature without having to trek into the mountains, this property is the one to book. This small pension, north of the Hotel Zlatorog on the Sava Bohinjka River, boasts just nine rooms. Slightly isolated, it can sometimes feel a little removed from the action, but is a perfect place for total peace and relaxation. Few amenities are on offer – just a basic, clean room in a tranquil setting. Discounts are available to youth and student cardholders. ⓐ Ukanc 128 ⓣ (04) 574 6400

Hotel Zlatorog ££ Situated in natural surroundings at the shore of the Sava river. ⓐ Ribcev laz 50 ⓣ (04) 577 8000

Soča Valley & Istrian Coast

These astonishingly beautiful areas were, for centuries, peaceful areas of rivers, cliffs and ravines. Now, those very natural features are turning the area into a magnet for sports fans, especially those of the extreme variety.

GETTING THERE

By road

Four buses a day departing every two hours (or so) leave Ljubljana bus station bound for Bovec. Depending on the road conditions, the journey can take anything from two to three hours. Drivers should follow the E61 motorway as far as Kranjska Gora and follow the signs to Borec. Be warned that, once off the motorway, the drive is filled with cliffside twists and turns. Nervous drivers and those afraid of heights need not apply. Idrija isn't accessible using the country's motorway system. The easiest option is to take the E61/70 motorway as far as Predama Castle, turn north on the secondary road and follow the signs.

BOVEC

Just 16 km (10 miles) away from the Italian border is this popular natural resort town considered to be the unofficial capital of the Soča Valley. Alpine enthusiasts adore the place, attracted by the wealth of sporting options, soaring mountains and crystal-clear lakes. The ski resort at Kamin is well-equipped and extensive, offering plenty of trails and runs to pack an extended stay. For a truly memorable experience, book a guided trip with one of the former goatherds into the surrounding hills. Tours can be arranged through the Tourist Information Office in the centre of town.

SIGHTS & ATTRACTIONS
Hiking & cycling
There are a number of stunning walks and hikes through the surrounding areas, with maps and guided trips available through

⬤ *White-water rafting down the Soča River*

the local tourist office. The most popular journey takes visitors to the Boka Waterfall, located to the southwest of town. For details and prices, contact the tourist office. ⓐ Trg Golobarskih žrtev 8 ① (05) 384 1919 ⓦ www.bovec.si

Rafting & canoeing

From April to October it is possible to rent a canoe or organise a rafting trip along the Soča River. Rafting trips can be organised on the day and usually take anywhere from two to eight people on a 10 km (6 mile) journey. Outfitters will include use of a life jacket, windbreaker, long johns, a paddle and helmet in the cost of the trip. Be sure to bring a swimsuit, T-shirt and a towel, as you are sure to get soaked. Kayak and canoe trips are usually done alone, with rentals on an hourly basis. No office or centre, just wander around.

Skiing

The mountains northeast of Bovec hold the Kamin ski centre, a high-altitude alpine centre with a long ski season that sometimes lasts into early May. Fifteen km (9 miles) of pistes and cross-country runs are on offer, served by chairs and T-bars. For non-athletes, a cable car runs all year, offering views of the valley below. For more information or to purchase ski passes at Kamin, call ① (05) 389 6310 ⓦ www.bovec.si

TAKING A BREAK

Gostišče Stari Kovač £ Every Slovenian town has its pizzeria. This is the local choice for Bovec. ⓐ Rupa 3 ① (05) 388 6699 ⓦ www.starikovac.com ⓛ Variable, so phone to check

AFTER DARK

Restaurants

Letni Vrt £ This casual eatery serves up grilled meats, fresh trout and, of course, pizza. Located across from the Alp Hotel, it's a nice place for a meal – especially during the summer months when the garden opens up to diners. ❸ Trg Golobarskih žrtev 1 ❶ (05) 389 6384 🕓 Variable, so phone to check

Martinov Hram £–££ Seafood and grilled meats are the speciality of this centrally located inn. ❸ Trg Golobarskih žrtev 27 ❶ (05) 388 6214 🕓 Variable, so phone to check

ACCOMMODATION

Apartments Gotour £–££ These apartments and rooms for active travellers are located in the centre of Bovec and provide access to all sorts of water sports on the Soča River. In winter the owners organise sledging as well as paragliding. ❸ Trg Golobarskih žrtev 50, Bovec ❶ (05) 389 6366 ❿ www.gotourbovec.com

Dobra Vila Bovec £–££ As they say themselves it's a place for spoilt bon vivants, adventuresome travellers and intellectual lazybones. A beautiful building in a wonderful setting. ❸ Mala vas 112 ❶ (05) 389 6400 ❿ www.dobra-vila-bovec.com

Pristava Lepena £–££ Cute holiday village set in an idyllic alpine meadow setting. While the complex is located 15 km (9 miles) southeast of town, it's perfect for those looking to immerse themselves in nature, rather than in town life. Rooms are located in six traditional houses divided into quaint apartments. ❸ Lepena 2 ❶ (05) 388 9900 ❿ www.levant.si

IDRIJA

Idrija is a picture-perfect locale nestled in a deep basin at the confluence of two rivers. Surrounded by green hills, it's renowned for its natural vistas and was once one of the richest towns in Slovenia, due to its once booming lace-making and mercury mining operations. In fact, 13 per cent of the world's mercury supply originated here during Idrija's peak. Idrija isn't the place to visit if your idea of a good time is pubs and parties. For a truly local experience, try and plan your trip to coincide with the annual lace-making festival in August.

SIGHTS & ATTRACTIONS
Anthony Mine Shaft

Live out your mining fantasies on this tour that allows you to experience what it was like to be a mercury miner during the town's heyday. The tour begins in an 18th-century call room where miners were assigned each morning to their daily duties. Here, you will watch an interesting 20-minute movie in English that describes the history of both the town and the mine that made it famous.

You will then have to put on heavy coats and helmets with attached torches before entering the shaft into the first mine, which was sunk in the year 1500.

The tour takes a circular journey, during which you will see examples of live mercury on the walls and cinnabar ore from which the metal is extracted. A chapel in the mine served the miners, dedicated to their patron saint, St Barbara. ⓐ Kosovelova ulica 3 ⓣ (05) 377 1142 ⓛ Tours: 10.00 & 15.00 Mon–Fri, 10.00 & 16.00 Sat & Sun, Dec–Mar; 10.00 & 15.00 Mon–Fri, 10.00, 15.00, 16.00 Sat & Sun, Apr–Nov

▶ Idyllic Idrija

Wild Lake

Follow the Idrija River Canal to Wild Lake, a lush lake fed by a clear karst spring. Following heavy rainfall, the pressure builds up underground forcing the water up like a geyser, giving the impression that the lake is boiling – it isn't. Declared a national monument by the Slovenian government in 1967, the lake's signboards outline details about native trees, plants and wildlife. On your stroll to the lake, be sure not to miss seeing the Kamsit – a water wheel that was used to pump water out of flooded mines for almost two centuries. It's located about 3 km (2 miles) to the north, about one-third of the journey from the old town.

CULTURE

Municipal Museum

The town of Idrija made its early fortunes on the back of its two major industries: mercury mining and lace-making. Both traditions are chronicled in detail at this intriguing local museum, which takes up three wings of a hilltop castle surrounding a courtyard.

During the 16th century, Idrija became a key centre of industry following the discovery that mercury could be used to separate gold and silver from rock. Town business boomed as a result and an extensive display dedicated to the heavy metal testifies to its importance to local townspeople.

The ethnographic collection tells the story of the miners who resided here, through various reconstructed rooms that detail their lifestyles through the years. A typical local salary up until the 1980s was double the national average, meaning that many luxuries could be afforded when compared to other communities.

A new exhibition exists on the second floor covering Idrija's modern-day history from the days of Italian occupation during

◆ *Idrija's local museum is housed in its castle*

World War I through to the early days of socialism and the birth of Yugoslavia. The massive hammer and sickle that dominates the room once hung over the mine entrance.

Finally there is also a large room outlining local lace-making traditions. Regionally produced lace is still valued and examples are highly sought after by collectors. ⓐ Prelovčeva ulica 9 ⓣ (05) 372 6600 ⓦ www.muzej-idrija-cerkno.si ⓛ 09.00–18.00

POTOROŽ – SEASIDE AND SPECIAL

Love it or hate it, Potorož is the seaside town of choice in Slovenia. Visitors would be forgiven for making the obvious comparisons to Blackpool or Benidorm, possibly confused by the tacky high-rise developments that line the coast – but locals love the place and flock to its sandy beaches whenever warm weather strikes.

A resort has existed at this location for centuries, as visitors have been drawn by the (supposedly) healing waters of its local spas. While there isn't much visually to speak of today, the spas remain active and retain their functional feel.

For a more graceful seaside holiday, go instead to the beautiful Venetian-era town of Piran just a few kilometres further up the coast. Not only is this village more visually striking, it also attracts Slovenia's glitterati, due to its truly unspoilt atmosphere. During the summer months, buses leave regularly from Ljubljana station. The E70 motorway takes drivers directly to the coastal resorts, but be warned that warm weekends can see legendarily bad traffic.

AFTER DARK

Restaurants

Gostilna Kos £ *Žlikrofi* is a local speciality that resembles ravioli and is stuffed with bacon, chives and potatoes. This pub dishes up the town's best examples – but you'd better be hungry because it's extraordinarily filling. ⓐ Tomšičeva ulica 4 ⓣ (05) 372 2030 ⓛ Variable, so phone to check

Pri Škafarju £ While there are tons of menu options, most locals stick to the tasty pizza made in the on-site wood-burning oven. ❷ Ulica Svete Barbare 9 ❶ (05) 377 3240 ◐ Variable, so phone to check

ACCOMMODATION

Dijaški Dom Nikolaj Pirnat £ Student dormitory close to the town centre. The multi-bed rooms are only available during the summer months. ❷ Ulica IX Korpusa 6 ❶ (05) 373 4070

Gostišče Barbara ££ Located directly above the entrance to the Anthony Mine Shaft (see page 116), this six-room property is standard and central. The boarding house also has a restaurant which is open from Monday to Friday from 16.00–22.00. ❷ Kosovelova ulica 3 ❶ (05) 377 1162

Hotel Kendov Dvorec ££–£££ For total romance, book yourself into the castle hotel located 4 km (2$^{1}/_{2}$ miles) north of town. There are only 12 rooms in this converted family mansion, which dates back to the 14th century. Guests can enjoy the antique 19th-century furnishings and views of the Idrijca Valley. Be sure to book yourself in for a meal at the hotel's Hana Room. Even if you aren't staying here, it's worth the trip. ❷ Spodnja Idrija ❶ (05) 372 5100 Ⓦ www.kendov-dvorec.com

Southern Slovenia

South of Ljubljana is a region of natural beauty, dotted with few towns and even fewer tourists. The main attractions are centred around the town of Postojna. However, the rolling hills and thick forests hold secret treasures in the form of beautiful rock formations, hidden monasteries, castles, spas, vineyards and delightful valleys carved out by ancient rivers. Known for its fruit-growing, folk traditions abound here, and celebrations can be found in various towns on weekends throughout the summer.

Cycling, hiking and camping possibilities are many, and the various towns offer great wine-tasting options for fans of the locally produced light red wine. Getting around this region is difficult, especially outside the main administrative centres. Bus and train services are limited, making a car a necessity if this region is top of your itinerary.

GETTING THERE

By road
Buses depart Ljubljana every half-hour to Postojna as they travel their way to the coast. The town is also on the main train line to Trieste. The journey takes about an hour. To drive, take the A1/E61/E70 motorway.

Ten buses and 15 trains serve Novo Mesto from Ljubljana every day, each taking about an hour. By car, take the E70/H1 motorway towards Croatia. Novo Mesto is located halfway between Ljubljana and Zagreb.

POSTOJNA

The town of Postojna isn't of particular interest, but serves as the jumping-off point for one of Slovenia's most visited sights – the Postojna Caves (see page 124). Highly forgettable, the town serves

🔺 Take a cave tour to see ancient stalactites

as the administrative centre for the region and should be avoided if visits to the caves and castle aren't in your plans. A stay of a day or two will cover all the sights with plenty of time to spare.

SIGHTS & ATTRACTIONS

Postojna Caves

Over 19 km (12 miles) of tunnels, chambers and passages make up the Postojna Cave system, which lies under a limestone plateau. The sight of forest-like stalagmites and stalactites is inspiring, formed by millions of years of erosion and rainfall seeping through the limestone ceiling.

Signatures carved into the walls date from 1213, but only became famous following a visit by Emperor Franz Ferdinand in 1819. An electric train has since been installed, taking visitors 4 km (2½ miles) into the heart of the system.

Cave tours can be extremely popular during summer. Try to go on either the first or last tour of the day to avoid the crowds, and be sure to dress warmly as the interior can get quite cold.

During the tour, the main attraction, in addition to the various chambers and formations, is a tank containing *Proteus anguinus* – the largest cave-dwelling vertebrate in the world. A bizarre-looking creature, it was originally mistaken for a dragon when first discovered by locals many centuries ago. ⓐ Jamska cesta 30 ⓣ (05) 700 0100 ⓦ www.postojna-cave.com ⓛ Variable, so phone to check

Predjama Castle

If not for the Postojna Caves, the Predjama Castle would easily be the most impressive sight in the region. Located 9 km (5½ miles)

● *The 'castle in the rock' at Predjama*

north of Postojna town, the castle stands in the mouth of a cavern halfway up a 123 m (404 ft) cliff. The result is high drama. While a castle has stood here since the 12th century, the present structure dates from the 16th century and includes a number of styles from Romanesque to Gothic.

The interiors of the castle are far less inspiring than the exterior, filled with eight reconstructed museum rooms. Be sure to examine the drawbridge, dungeon and secret passage entrance.

LAKE CERKNICA

Located east of Postojna is Lake Cerknica, a 'disappearing' lake that has been written about since the days of the Greek Empire. The lake is only a lake during short periods, created when the area floods during the autumn and spring. Fed by waters from the plateaus to the east and mountains to the west, the lake can be created over the course of just a few days. At its largest, it can grow to 10 km (6 miles) in length and 5 km (3 miles) wide. As the drier summer months approach, the lake slowly disappears into the sinkholes and potholes on which the lake is located, taking as long as three to four weeks to finally be erased until the next rainy season. For a better understanding of how the lake works, include a visit to the Museum of Lake Cerknica in the town of Dolenje Jezero. Exhibits include live bird recordings, a 25-minute slide show of lake images and a model of local canoes, used until as recently as 1970 to transport livestock across the water. ❸ Dolenje Jezero 1e ❶ (01) 709 4053 ❾ www.jezerski-hram.si ❹ 15.00 Sat only. Tours at other times can be arranged by calling in advance

Of greater interest are the caves below the castle. Only 900 m (2,953 ft) are available for exploration, and as the path is only partially constructed and there is no lighting installed, boots and a torch are required. ⓐ Predjamski Grad ⓣ (05) 700 0100 ⓦ www.postojna-cave.com ⓛ 11.00, 13.00, 15.00, 17.00 May–Sept, closed Oct–Apr

TAKING A BREAK

Pizzeria Minutka £ Local pizzeria with an outdoor terrace popular with locals. ⓐ Ljubljanska cesta 14 ⓣ (05) 720 3625 ⓛ Variable, so phone to check

AFTER DARK

Restaurants

Jadran ££ Centrally located 'old-fashioned' eatery that's strong on fish dishes. ⓐ Titov trg 1 ⓣ (05) 720 3900 ⓛ Variable, so phone to check

Restavracija Jamska ££ Located at the entrance to the caves and featuring a selection of eight set menus. The 1920s-style building provides pleasant surroundings. ⓐ Jamska cesta 28 ⓣ (05) 700 0181 ⓛ Variable, so phone to check

Bars, clubs & discos

Bar Bor There aren't that many party options in this sleepy town. Bar Bor stands out due to its central location. ⓐ Tržaška cesta 4a ⓣ (05) 726 4230 ⓛ Variable, so phone to check

ACCOMMODATION

Bike Hotel Sport £–££ A 3-star hotel located near the centre of town and very near the Postojna Caves. Modern and standard rooms offer

all amenities necessary for cyclists such as bike storage, hire, etc.
🅐 Kolodvorska ulica 1 🅣 (05) 720 2244 🅦 www.sport-hotel.si

Hotel Jama £–££ This mid-to-large hotel is convenient only if
explorations of Postojna Caves are a top priority. Just 200 m
(656 ft) southeast of the cave entrance, it's a bit of a trek to
the town centre. 🅐 Jamska cesta 28 🅣 (05) 700 0100
🅦 www.postojna-cave.com

NOVO MESTO

The town of Novo Mesto is the largest in southeast Slovenia and
has been an important cultural and economic centre since the
Middle Ages. The region has been continuously settled since the
Bronze Age, and numerous archaeological sites attest to this fact.
Today, it has a strong industrial base, housing both pharmaceutical
and automotive factories. While sights are limited, it's a convenient
jumping-off point for explorations of the surrounding hills and
spas – and the museum with its extensive collection of artefacts
is fascinating for fans of the Bronze and Middle Ages.

SIGHTS & ATTRACTIONS
Chapter Church of St Nicholas
This church is the town's oldest monument, designed using a mish-
mash of Gothic, neo-Gothic and baroque architectural elements.
While the 15th-century presbytery is the most celebrated feature
of the church, there are also a number of intriguing works of art,
including a Tintoretto – one of only two in the entire country.
🅐 Kapiteljski hrib 🅛 Variable; keys can be obtained from the
Provost's House on Kapiteljska ulica 1

◯ *Mesmerising sculptures on the Chapter Church of St Nicholas*

Glavni trg

The main square of the old town is home to the neo-Renaissance city hall, and was once the address of choice for craftsmen and merchants. Other buildings located nearby include St Leonard's Franciscan church, visible due to its classy yellow gabled façade, the adjoining monastery and Jakac House, with its collection of sketches and drawings created by Slovenian artist Božidar Jakac.

CULTURE

Dolenjska Museum

Located in a building that once housed the Knights of the Teutonic Order, this large museum holds a strong collection of archaeological finds that were unearthed during the late 1960s. The most important artefact is the Hallstatt helmet, dating from 800 BC, with two axe blows carved into the top. Other exhibits examine recent and ethnographic history, with a strong focus on World War II partisans. ⓐ Muzejska ulica 7 ⓣ (07) 373 1130 ⓦ www.dolmuzej.com ⓛ 08.00–17.00 Tues–Sat, 09.00–13.00 Sun, closed Mon

TAKING A BREAK

Picerija Tratnik Slovenia loves its pizzerias and Novo Mesto is no exception. This eatery is the most central one to enjoy a slice or two. ⓐ Glavni trg 11 ⓣ (07) 497 5079 ⓛ Variable, so phone to check

AFTER DARK

Restaurants

Restavracija Breg £–££ Back in its day, this restaurant was a favoured dining spot for Slovenia's artists and intelligentsia. Savvy bohemians still come here to enjoy the hearty local specialities, including bottles of the light Slovenian red wine produced in the region. In warmer months, meals can be enjoyed in the garden. ❸ Cvelbarjeva 9 ❶ (07) 332 1269 ❶ Variable, so phone to check

Tsing Tao £–££ Chinese cuisine in a small Slovenian town? Surprisingly, it's actually pretty good. Dishes are simple and don't stray far from the usual options. ❸ Dilančeva ulica 7 ❶ (07) 332 4388 ❶ Variable, so phone to check

Bars, clubs & discos
Pri Slonu Cosy pub, popular with the local student and artist crowd. Less raucous than most. ❸ Rozmanova ulica 22 ❶ (07) 332 1495 ❶ 19.00–01.00

Cinemas & theatres
House of Culture This local cinema offers screenings every night at 20.00 and sponsors occasional live music and theatre performances. ❸ Prešernov trg 3 ❶ (07) 332 1214

ACCOMMODATION
Hotel pri Belokranjcu £–££ This family hotel is situated in the centre of town. Here you can sip *Cvicek*, a wine that's typical in the Dolenjska region. Rooms are basic and standard. ❸ Kandijska cesta 63 ❶ (07) 302 8444 ❶ www.pribelokranjcu-vp.si

Hotel Grad Otocec ££–£££ Ever fancied kipping in a 13th-century medieval castle that's been done up luxuriously? Oh, yes. ❸ Grajska cesta 1 ❶ (07) 307 5699 ❶ www.terme-krka.si/en/otocec/grad

Eastern Slovenia

While this area doesn't boast the well-known attractions and sights west of Ljubljana, it does have quaint countryside towns and picture-perfect nature spots. In spring and summer, the region comes into its own with a number of music, dance and folk festivals.

Maribor and Celje (the second- and third-largest cities in Slovenia, see pages 133 & 136) provide the economic backbone for the region, but pale sights-wise to the more appealing tourist spots of the rural respites that surround them, specifically the town of Ptuj (see page 139).

Eastern Slovenia is well known for its wine producing and natural spas. Spend your days soaking in the healing waters and your nights imbibing the various vintages.

GETTING THERE

By rail
Maribor is also on the main train line linking Celje with Vienna and Graz. From Ljubljana, the journey time is 90 minutes by express train.

By road
Up to eight buses service Maribor from Ljubljana every day, with additional daily services available to Austria, Germany and Croatia. By car from Ljubljana, take motorway E57/A1.

To get to Ptuj from Ljubljana, travel to Maribor and then take one of the regular weekday bus services. On weekends, travel is limited, so plan in advance. Bus journeys may include a change in Maribor and take three hours to reach the town. Drivers should follow the E57/A1 motorway in the direction of Maribor, and exit at Slovenska Bistrica, following signs to Ptuj.

Celje can be reached by hourly bus services from Ljubljana, taking about 1¼ hours to complete the journey. If you are driving, take the E57/A1 motorway directly to the city.

MARIBOR

Slovenia's second-largest city, it feels like a small town when compared with the capital. The old Austrianate centre has a number of churches

◆ *Sculpture in the castle at Maribor*

and squares and it's a great jumping-off point for Slovenian nature tours. To the north lie great wineries, while hiking and camping opportunities abound to the south at the Pohorje Massif.

SIGHTS & ATTRACTIONS
Cathedral
The dominant building on Slomškov trg is the 13th-century cathedral dedicated to St John the Baptist. Architectural styles range from Romanesque to neo-Gothic. ⓐ Slomškov trg

Maribor Castle
Located on the northeast corner of Maribor's main Old Town square, this castle was built in the 15th century over a medieval fortress. The interiors combine baroque and rococo features. ⓐ Grajski trg 2 ⓘ (02) 228 3551 ⓛ 09.00–17.00 Tues–Sat, 10.00–14.00 Sun, closed Mon

Synagogue
To the west of the city's old water tower is a series of steps leading to Židovska ulica (Jewish Street) and the city's Jewish district. In addition to the square Jewish Tower, which now holds a photo gallery, is the restored 15th-century synagogue. ⓐ Židovska ulica 4 ⓘ (02) 252 7836 ⓛ 07.30–14.30 Mon–Fri, closed Sat & Sun

CULTURE
Maribor Regional Museum
The ground floor features archaeological, clothing and ethnographic exhibits, while the second floor offers Greek, Roman and Jewish artefacts, in addition to examples of local arts and crafts. ⓐ Pokrajinski Muzej Maribor, Maribor Castle, Grajski trg 2 ⓘ (02) 228 3551

Ⓦ www.pmuzej-mb.si 🕐 09.00–16.00 Tues–Sat, 09.00–14.00 Sun, closed Mon

TAKING A BREAK

Gledališka Kavarna £ Bohemians, artists and the local gay crowd congregate at this 'Theatre Café', located next to the Slovenian National Theatre. ⓐ Slovenska ulica 27 ⓣ (02) 252 3720 🕐 Variable, so phone to check

AFTER DARK

Restaurants

Gotišče Pri Treh Ribnikih ££ Also known as the 'Inn of the Three Fishponds', this restaurant is a country-style eatery in the middle of City Park. Dishes are heavy and filling, featuring dumplings and plenty of pork. ⓐ Ribniška ulica 9 ⓣ (02) 234 4170 🕐 Variable, so phone to check

Bars, clubs & discos

Jazz Club Satchmo Live jazz club located in the cellar of the Fine Arts Gallery. ⓐ Strossmayerjeva ulica 6 ⓣ (02) 250 2150 Ⓦ www.jazz-klub.si 🕐 Variable, so phone to check

Patrick's Pub Lively and authentic-feeling place to quench your thirst. Attracts a lively crowd. ⓐ Poštna ulica 10 ⓣ (02) 251 1801 Ⓦ robot.domovanje.com 🕐 Variable, so phone to check

Cinemas & theatres

Maribor Puppet Theatre Year-round puppet performances for both children and adults. ⓐ Ratovški trg 2 ⓣ (02) 228 1970 Ⓦ www.lg-mb.si 🕐 Opening times vary, so check listings

Slovenian National Theatre Maribor Ballet, theatre and opera performances. ➌ Slovenska ulica 27 ➊ (02) 250 6115 Ⓦ www.sng-mb.si ⏰ Box office: 10.00–15.00 Mon–Fri, until 13.00 Sat and two hours before each performance

ACCOMMODATION

Uni Hotel £ This hostel is centrally located in Maribor and attached to the Orel Hotel. In this way you get the benefits of staying in a hotel rather than a hostel for hostel prices. ➌ Volkmerjev prehod 7 ➊ (02) 2506 700

Orel Hotel £–££ For location, this hotel can't be beaten – but it needs a lick of paint. ➌ Volkmerjev prehod 7 ➊ (02) 250 6700 Ⓦ www.termemb.si

Hotel Bellevue ££–£££ This hotel is situated on the Mariborkso Pohorje plateau and has very good views. ➌ Na Slemenu 35 ➊ (02) 607 5100

CELJE

This industrial city has been around since Roman times. The Old Town has a number of buildings of interest to architecture buffs, such as Krekov trg with the neo-Gothic Celje Hall, a medieval defence tower and a Water Tower; Slomškov trg's 14th-century Abbey Church of St Daniel; Glavni trg, which is considered to be the heart of the Old Town; and Breg, a street on the south bank of the Savinja River leading to the Capuchin Church of St Cecilia.

SIGHTS & ATTRACTIONS
Šempeter
This town, 12 km (7¹/₂ miles) west of Celje, houses a Roman necropolis that was reconstructed between 1952 and 1966. ⓐ Rimska nekropola ⓘ (03) 700 2056 ⓦ www.td-sempeter.si ⓛ 10.00–18.00 Apr–Sept; 10.00–16.00 Sat & Sun, closed Mon–Fri, Oct–Mar

Stari Grad Celje (Celje Old Castle)
This 13th-century castle is the largest fortress in Slovenia. Located 2 km (1 mile) southeast of the Old Town, it sits high on an escarpment overlooking the region. ⓐ Grajski hrib ⓘ (03) 548 1777

CULTURE
Celje Regional Museum
Skulls of 18 of its former counts are displayed in glass cabinets, but the main attraction is a ceiling known as the *Celjski Strop* (Celje Ceiling), which was painted in the early 17th century by an anonymous Polish artist. ⓐ Muzejski trg 1 ⓘ (03) 428 0950 ⓦ www.pokmuz-ce.si ⓛ 10.00–18.00 Tues–Sun, closed Mon

Museum of Recent History
Located in the former town-hall building, this museum chronicles Celje from the late 19th century to the present day. ⓐ Prešernova ulica 17 ⓘ (03) 4286 410 ⓛ 10.00–18.00 Mon–Fri, 09.00–12.00 Sat, 14.00–18.00 Sun ⓦ www.muzej-nz-ce.si

TAKING A BREAK
Gostilnica Tartini £ Attractive lunch stop convenient for those visiting the museum. Typical, café-style sandwiches and local dishes. ⓐ Glavni trg 12 ⓘ (03) 425 5550 ⓛ Variable, so phone to check

AFTER DARK
Restaurants
Gostilna Amerika £ Huge dishes of Southern Balkan specialities including vegetable stews and skewered meats. ⓐ Mariborska cesta 79 ⓣ (03) 541 9320 ⓦ www.gostilna-amerika.com ⓛ Variable, so phone to check

Istrska Konoba ££ Probably Celje's fanciest restaurant. Also known as the 'Istrian Cellar', the interiors were designed by karst artist Lojze Spacal. The doors and windows feature stunning examples of stained glass. ⓐ Gledališka ulica 7 ⓣ (03) 548 4611 ⓛ Variable, so phone to check

Bars, clubs & discos
Branibor Pub Live music and jazz pub. Good for a chilled evening out. ⓐ Satnetova ulica 29 ⓣ (03) 492 4144 ⓛ Variable, so phone to check

Cinemas & theatres
Slovenski Ljudsko Gledališče (Slovenian People's Theatre)
Considered one of the best professional theatres in Slovenia, this venue hosts the Days of Comedy festival in February. ⓐ Gledališka ulica 5 ⓣ (03) 4264 200 ⓛ Box office: 09.00–11.00, 17.00–19.00 Mon–Fri, also 60 minutes prior to each performance

ACCOMMODATION
Hotel Faraon £–££This hotel is situated in a tranquil part of Celje, near the promenade of the Savinja River and close to the old town centre. ⓐ Ljubljanska cesta 39 ⓣ (03) 545 2018

Hotel Evropa ££ Clean, comfortable and modern rooms conveniently located close to the train station. ⓐ Krekov trg 4 ⓣ (03) 426 9000 ⓦ www.hotel-evropa.si

Turška Mačka ££ Also known as the 'Turkish Cat', this hotel is the cheapest in town (other than the student accommodation). Rooms are slightly gloomy, but serviceable. ⓐ Gledališka ulica 7 ⓣ (03) 548 4611

PTUJ

Equal to Ljubljana in historical importance, the town of Ptuj is one of Slovenia's oldest towns. The compact medieval core is dominated by the hilltop castle northwest of the centre.

SIGHTS & ATTRACTIONS

Drava Tower
Built in the 16th century, the Renaissance water tower was built to help defend the town from the Turks. Today, it houses a gallery dedicated to the works of graphic artist France Mihelič. ⓐ Dracska ulica 4 ⓛ 10.00–13.00, 16.00–19.00 Tues–Fri, closed Sat–Mon

Ptuj Castle
Built in the early 12th century, it has a fascinating collection of musical instruments dating back to the 17th century. The first floor features period rooms of portraits, weapons, furniture and tapestries. The top floor is dedicated to Gothic art. ⓐ Na Gradu 1 ⓣ (02) 748 9230, (02) 748 0350 ⓛ 09.00–17.00 mid-Oct–May; 09.00–18.00 June, Sept–mid-Oct; 09.00–18.00 Mon–Fri, 09.00–20.00 Sat & Sun, July & Aug

⬤ *Ptuj overlooks the Drava River*

Slovenski trg

Considered the heart of Ptuj, this street houses the bulk of the town's most celebrated buildings. Structures to check out include the local theatre, a Roman 'Orpheus Monument' dating from the second century AD and a tower built in the 16th century that acted as a watchtower.

CULTURE

Ptuj Regional Museum

Housed in the former Dominican Monastery inside Ptuj Castle, the museum's highlights include lapidary and archaeological exhibits.

MINORITE MONASTERY

This massive working monastery was built in the 13th century and escaped the Habsburg religious dissolution edicts. On the first floor is a summer refectory featuring stucco work, and ceiling paintings chronicling the lives of St Peter and St Paul. There is also a stunning library of 5,000 manuscripts including an original copy of the New Testament from the mid-16th century.

The northern side of the monastery is dominated by the Church of Saints Peter and Paul – once considered to be the finest example of Gothic architecture in Slovenia. 🅐 Minoritski trg 1 🕿 (02) 771 3091 🕓 Open by appointment only

🅐 Muzejski trg 1 🕿 (02) 787 9230 🕓 09.00–17.00 mid-Oct–May; 09.00–18.00 June, Sept–mid-Oct; 09.00–18.00 Mon–Fri, 09.00–20.00 Sat & Sun, July & Aug 🌐 www.pok-muzej-ptuj.si

TAKING A BREAK

Grajska Kavarna £ Great café serving light drinks and snacks. A nice place for a lunch or coffee break. 🅐 Na Gradu 1 🕿 (02) 787 9230 🕓 Variable, so phone to check

AFTER DARK

Restaurants

Ribič £–££ Delightful fish restaurant that offers local river catches, including delicious trout and seafood soup. 🅐 Dravska ulica 9 🕿 (02) 749 0635 🕓 Variable, so phone to check

Bars, clubs & discos

Café Evropa By day, this café is a popular locale for a pint and a pizza. On weekends it becomes the hottest club in town. ❸ Mestni trg 2 ❶ (02) 771 01235 ❾ www.evropa-pub.si ❸ Variable, so phone to check

Teater Kamra Caffè On weekdays, this café attracts a bohemian crowd. Weekends offer live music, including rock, folk and jazz. ❸ Prešernova ulica 6 ❶ (02) 787 7455 ❸ Variable, so phone to check

Cinemas & theatres

Kino Ptuj Art and mainstream movies shown at a jewel-like art deco filmhouse. ❸ Cvetkov trg 3 ❶ (02) 748 1810

ACCOMMODATION

Dom Ptuj – Mladinsko prenocisce £ This hostel is situated in the town centre near the railway and bus station. Each room has its own bathroom. ❸ Osojnikova 9 ❶ (02) 771 0814 ❾ www.csod.si

Hotel Roskar £–££ Situated near Ptuj, the kitchen here offers traditional Slovene food. ❸ Hajdose 43c ❶ (02) 782 3201

Garni Hotel Mitra ££–£££ Large rooms and a superb location make this hotel the best option in town. ❸ Prešernova ulica 6 ❶ (02) 787 7455 ❾ www.hotel-mitra.si

❿ *Getting around in Slovenia is not a problem*

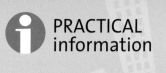

PRACTICAL
information

Directory

GETTING THERE

By air

For those planning a short stay, flying is the quickest and most convenient way to get to Ljubljana. The main entry point for scheduled flights into Slovenia is Ljubljana Jože Pučnik Airport (see below), otherwise known as Brnik Airport, which is served by the Slovenian flag carrier, **Adria Airways** (Ⓦ www.adria.si), a limited number of mostly Eastern European airlines and low-cost carrier **easyJet** (Ⓦ www.easyjet.com). Located 27 km (17 miles) northwest of the city, it's a basic facility providing exchange services. Travellers from the US will need to change planes in a European hub (most likely London, Paris or Munich) before reaching their final destination, as there are no non-stop services from North America. The average flying time from London is two hours, and it's nine hours from New York, including connections. Two other airports, **Maribor** (Ⓦ www.maribor-airport.si) and **Portorož** (Ⓦ www.portoroz-airport.si), are rarely used by foreign travellers, although Ryanair began a service in 2007 from Maribor to London. **Jože Pučnik Airport** Ⓐ Aerodrom Ljubljana, Zg. Brnik 130a Ⓦ www.lju-airport.si Ⓔ info@lju-airport.si

Many people are aware that air travel emits CO_2, which contributes to climate change. You may be interested in the possibility of lessening the environmental impact of your flight through the charity Climate Care, which offsets your CO_2 by funding environmental projects around the world. Visit Ⓦ www.climatecare.org

By rail

The journey by rail will involve two train changes – once in Paris from the Eurostar and again in Venice or Munich. The total journey time is approximately 12–16 hours, depending on connections. This as well as the price can vary. The monthly Thomas Cook European Rail Timetable has up-to-date schedules for European international and domestic train services.

Eurostar reservations ☎ (UK) (08705) 186 186 Ⓦ www.eurostar.com
Thomas Cook European Rail Timetable ☎ (UK) 01733 416 477 (USA) 1 800 322 3834 Ⓦ www.thomascookpublishing.com

By road

Roads in Slovenia are well maintained, but on the narrow side. While the journey from London is pleasant, it is on the long side, at 1,500 km (932 miles) in length. If you are considering extensive travel around Slovenia, then a car can be a good option.

Once across the channel, the most direct route is via Brussels, Stuttgart, Munich and Salzburg, before crossing into Slovenia at the Karavanke Tunnel. Journey time is approximately 16 hours without stops.

The country has a high level of car ownership, but roads remain relatively traffic-free. Snarls can occur in Ljubljana city centre, but they are nothing when compared to the problems of larger European capitals. Distances between destinations in Slovenia tend to be very short. Heavy snowfall can cause problems, especially in the Julian Alps. To drive in Slovenia, a driving licence and third-party insurance are required.

Slovenian traffic drives on the right and the speed limit is 130 kph (80 mph) on motorways, 90 kph (60 mph) on secondary or tertiary roads, and 50 kph (30 mph) in cities and towns. The most important road rules to adhere to while in the country are the prohibition against sounding the horn in built-up areas (unless in order to avoid an accident), and using a mobile phone while driving. Seatbelt use is compulsory, a triangular breakdown sign, reflective jacket and first aid kit must be kept in the car at all times, and dipped headlights must be switched on at all times throughout the day. Winter tyres are mandatory between 15th November and 15th March.

If you prefer to travel by bus or coach, Eurolines, the main bus company operating European coaches from London, now operates services to Ljubljana as well as Maribor in eastern Slovenia. The journey time is 28 hours and involves a change in Frankfurt. A standard return fare is £160.

Eurolines ☎ (08705) 143 219 🌐 www.eurolines.co.uk

ENTRY FORMALITIES

Visitors to Slovenia who are citizens of the UK, Ireland, Australia, the US, Canada, Israel or Japan will need a passport, but not a visa, for stays of up to 90 days. South African nationals do require a visa. If you are travelling from other countries, you may need a visa and it is best to check before you leave home.

Since Slovenia joined the Schengen Agreement in December 2007, border posts and checks have been removed between Italy and Austria. This has increased the custom controls with Croatia and Hungary. If travelling with a pet they must have a passport containing details of a valid rabies vaccination. Visitors can bring in, or take out, goods without restrictions on quantity or value, as long as these goods are for personal use only.

Other items that are duty-free include: 200 cigarettes (100 cigarillos, 50 cigars or 150 g of tobacco), 2 l of wine and 1 l of spirits, and 50 g of perfume. The import or export of more than €10,000 is forbidden unless permission has been obtained from the Bank of Slovenia.

As entry requirements and customs regulations are subject to change, you should always check the current situation with your local travel agent, airline or a Slovenian embassy or consulate before you leave.

MONEY

The currency in Slovenia is the euro, which replaced the Slovenian tolar (SIT) in 2007. In many places you will still find the prices listed in tolar as well as euro. You can withdraw money from ATMs at many Slovenian banks. Credit cards are widely accepted but some smaller businesses, including some restaurants, taverns, hotels and most market stalls, do not accept credit card payment. This is especially

🔺 Bus routes connect the city to the countryside

true outside Ljubljana and the main tourist destinations. It is advisable always to carry a small amount of cash to cover your day's purchases.

HEALTH, SAFETY & CRIME

It is not necessary to take any special health precautions while travelling in Slovenia. Tap water is safe to drink, but do not drink any water from surrounding lakes or rivers. Many Slovenians prefer bottled mineral water.

If you are going to do a lot of walking in forested areas, it is necessary to be careful of ticks. These blood-sucking parasites can transmit dangerous viral infections, along with various bacterial diseases. A good deterrent is the insecticide permethrin, sprinkled over your clothes. It is also wise to avoid walking through long grass with bare legs. In any case, after a walk always check your body for ticks. If you find one, remove it immediately with a pair of tick tweezers. These can be bought at pharmacies. Ask how to use them when buying. If a rash develops from a bite, consult a doctor immediately.

Pharmacies (or *lekarna*) are present throughout Ljubljana and most other Slovenian communities. Opening hours are usually from 07.30 to 19.00 Monday to Friday and on Saturday mornings until 13.00. A sign in the door will notify you as to the location of the nearest 24-hour pharmacy, should you need something in an emergency. Slovenian pharmacists are always well stocked and staff can provide expert advice.

Slovenian health care is of a good standard, but it is not free. EU citizens are entitled to reduced-cost, sometimes free, medical treatment that becomes necessary while travelling in Slovenia, on presentation of their European Health Insurance Card, or EHIC,

(Ⓦ www. ehic.org.uk). In most cases your travel insurance should provide the coverage you need.

As in any other big cities, crime is a fact of life in Ljubljana. Petty theft (bag-snatching, pick-pocketing) is the most common form of trouble; however, you are unlikely to experience violence or assault. Never leave valuables lying openly in your car, and always lock it. Strolling around the inner city at night is fairly safe, but avoid dimly lit streets. Your hotel will warn you about particularly dangerous or unwelcoming areas – but there really are very few.

When using public transport or walking on the street, carry your wallet in your front pocket, keep bags closed at all times, never leave valuables on the ground when you are seated at a table and always wear camera bags and purses crossed over your chest.

For emergency numbers, see 'Emergencies' on page 154.

OPENING HOURS

Most shops and department stores open Monday to Friday 08.00 –19.00, until 13.00 on Saturdays. Stores generally do not open on Sundays or public holidays. Weekend opening hours are not conducive to weekend short-breakers with a love of retail therapy. If you really want to shop, the BTC shopping centre (see page 22), located 3 km (2 miles) from the city centre, stays open until 20.00 on Saturdays. Banks open Monday to Friday 08.00–16.00 or 18.00, some with a one- or two-hour lunch break at some point during the day. A few major branches will also open from 08.00–13.00 on Saturdays.

Cultural institutions close for one day per week – usually Mondays. Standard hours are 10.00–18.00 from April to October. During the winter months, this schedule may be shortened, or may be reduced to weekends only. Pubs, bars, clubs and restaurants often work to ad hoc opening times, and it's always a wise idea to phone ahead. Usual post office opening hours are 08.00-19.00 Monday to Friday and Saturday 08.00–12.00 or 13.00.

TOILETS

Slovenia isn't exactly blessed with copious public lavatory facilities. When in doubt, head for the nearest train station, shopping centre or department store. Standards of hygiene are usually pretty good, but you will need to pay around €0.20 in the city centre for the pleasure.

Alternatively, try asking at one of the local cafés or bars. You may sometimes be expected to make a token purchase of coffee or water for the experience.

CHILDREN

Slovenia is generally a child-friendly place and no special health precautions need be taken for children, other than the above. Most restaurants, including the fanciful ones, welcome children. In some of the more 'neighbourhood' restaurants, there is usually a kids' menu. High chairs and cots come as standard at most dining establishments and hotels, but it's wise to book ahead.

Nappies and other baby necessities are readily obtained from supermarkets, and *lekarna* (pharmacies). Remember that weekend opening hours are extremely limited (see page 149), so be sure to purchase all your weekend baby needs in advance.

There are plenty of attractions in and around Ljubljana that will keep the kids occupied, but if the numerous museums and historic sights prove to be a little overwhelming, consider taking them to the Maribor Puppet Theatre (see page 135). Alternatively, take a stroll through the BTC City shopping centre (see page 22), where there are lots of child-focused diversions.

COMMUNICATION

Internet

Internet access is provided by some libraries and internet cafés around the city. One of the most popular cafés is:

Cyber Café Xplorer Ⓐ Petkovškovo nabrežje 23 🛈 (01) 430 1991

NeoWlan and Wi-Fi are available in many cafes and hotels in the town centre but they are rarely free of charge.

Phone

Coin-operated public phones do not exist. If you want to make a call from a public telephone in Slovenia, you will need a telephone card known as a *telefonska kartica*, or *telekartica* for short. Telephone cards can be bought at any post office and some news-stands. Phonecards cost from €5 to €25, depending on the number of units on the card. Cards come with 25, 50, 100 or 300 units.

Instructions on how to use public telephones are written in English in phone booths for international calls. Otherwise, lift up the receiver, insert the telephone card and dial the number.

Post

Postal services are quick and efficient. There are many post offices throughout the city, but the most convenient locations can be found at Slovenska 32 and Trg Osvobodilne Fronte 5. Stamps can be bought at post offices and there are rarely any long queues. If you don't find yourself close to a post office, some news-stands also sell both items. Post boxes are yellow. Letters weighing less than 20 g are €0.45 or €0.92 for up to 100 g. Postcards cost €0.35 to send. The airmail charge on top of all the above amounts is €0.25. It is wise to make the investment.

TELEPHONING SLOVENIA

The code to dial Slovenia from abroad, after the access code (oo in most countries), is 386. To call Ljubljana from within Slovenia dial (o1) and then the number, unless calling within Ljubljana itself, when there is no need to dial o1.

TELEPHONING ABROAD

When making an international call, dial the international code you require and drop the initial zero of the area code you are ringing. The international dialling code for calls from Slovenia to Australia is +61; to the UK +44; to the Irish Republic +353; to South Africa +27; to New Zealand +64; and to the USA and Canada +1.

ELECTRICITY

The standard electrical current is 220 volts. Two-pin adaptors can be purchased at most electrical shops.

TRAVELLERS WITH DISABILITIES

Facilities for visitors with disabilities are generally quite poor in Slovenia. The country has been slow to catch up with the needs of disabled travellers and still has a long way to go. Few locations are well equipped or even have basic facilities, and access to hotels and public buildings is impossible in many cases.

Facilities for visitors with disabilities arriving at the city's main international airport are good, though travellers with special needs should inform their airlines in advance. The **InterCity Slovenije** (ⓦ www.slo-zeleznice.si) trains between Ljubljana and Maribor have also joined the 21st century in introducing wheelchair facilities, specially adapted toilets, and access ramps to the platforms.

A useful source of advice when in Slovenia is **Zveza Paraplegikov Slovenije** (ⓐ Štihova ulica 14 ❶ (01) 432 7138 ⓦ www.zveza-paraplegikov.si).

Useful websites include:

ⓦ www.sath.org (US site).

ⓦ www.access-able.com (general advice on worldwide travel).

ⓦ http://travel.guardian.co.uk (UK site offering tips and links for disabled travellers).

TOURIST INFORMATION

Ljubljana's main tourist office is extremely helpful and shares its space with the Slovenian Tourist Board – so you can get information on the entire country in one convenient location. Maps and information are available free of charge in English.

Ljubljana Tourist Information Centre ⓐ Adamič-Lundrovo nabrežje 2 ❶ (01) 306 1215 ⓦ www.ljubljana.si/en/tourism ❶ 08.00–21.00 June–Sept; 08.00–19.00 Oct–May

BACKGROUND READING

The City and the Child by Ales Debeljak. Contemporary poetry anthology by a modern-day master.

Slovenia & the Slovenes by Cathie Carmichael and James Gow. Comprehensive exploration of 20th-century Slovenian history, culture, economics and politics.

The Sonnets of Unhappiness by France Prešeren. Beautiful poetry from the early 19th century by Slovenia's most iconic literary figure.

Emergencies

The following are emergency free call numbers:

Ambulance ☎ 112
Fire brigade ☎ 112
Police ☎ 113

MEDICAL SERVICES

The British Embassy (see page 155) has a list of English-speaking doctors; however, most doctors in Ljubljana speak at least the basics. Make sure that you have a European Health Insurance Card (if you are from the EU, see page 148) and/or private travel insurance.

There is an emergency medical centre at the **Klinični Center** (ⓐ Zaloška 2 ☎ (01) 552 5050). A duty daytime dentist is available (ⓐ Kotnikova 36 ☎ (01) 300 9674) and a duty night time dentist (ⓐ Metelkova 9 ☎ (01) 472 3700).

Prescription and non-prescription drugs (including aspirin) are only sold at pharmacies (*lekarna*). Most keep standard business hours, which are 07.30–19.00 Mon–Fri and until 13.00 Sat. A list of pharmacies open on Sundays and in the evening should be displayed near the door of every pharmacy.

Two reliable hospitals are:

Klinični Centre Ljubljana ⓐ Zaloška 2 ☎ (01) 552 5050
Zdravstveni Dom Health Center ⓐ Metelkova 9 ☎ (01) 472 3700

POLICE

The Slovenian capital is a relatively safe city with a low crime rate. However, sensible precautions should be taken. Take valuables with you whenever you leave your car unattended, cross purse and satchel straps over the body when walking, and keep wallets in the front pocket of trousers. If you do become a victim, report the crime immediately at the central police station (📍 Trdinova 10 📞 (01) 475 0600).

Lost property

For items lost on buses, contact the **LPP Information Centre** (📍 Celoš ka 160 📞 (01) 582 2420). For items lost on trains, check with the information counter at Ljubljana station, and for property left in taxis, contact the office of the taxi company you used.

EMBASSIES & CONSULATES

Australian Consulate 📍 Dunajska cesta 50 📞 (01) 425 4252
British Embassy 📍 Trg Republike 3/IV 📞 (01) 200 3910
🌐 www.british-embassy.si
Canadian Consulate 📍 Dunajska cesta 22 📞 (01) 430 3570
Irish Embassy 📍 Palača Kapitelj, Poljanski nasip 6 📞 (01) 300 8970
New Zealand Consulate 📍 Verovškova 57 📞 (01) 580 3055
Republic of South Africa Consulate 📍 Pražakova 4 📞 (01) 200 6300
US Embassy 📍 Prešernova 31 📞 (01) 200 5500

EMERGENCY PHRASES

Help!	**Fire!**	**Stop!**
Na pomoč!	Gori!	Stop!
Na pomoch!	*Goree!*	*Stop!*

Call an ambulance/a doctor/the police/the fire brigade!
Pokličite rešilca/zdravnika/policijo/gasilce!
Pokleecheeteh resheeltsa/zdrowneeka/poleetseeyo/gaseeltse!

INDEX

WHAT'S IN YOUR GUIDEBOOK?

Independent authors Impartial up-to-date information from our travel experts who meticulously source local knowledge.

Experience Thomas Cook's 165 years in the travel industry and guidebook publishing enriches every word with expertise you can trust.

Travel know-how Contributions by thousands of staff around the globe, each one living and breathing travel.

Editors Travel-publishing professionals, pulling everything together to craft a perfect blend of words, pictures, maps and design.

You, the traveller We deliver a practical, no-nonsense approach to information, geared to how you really use it.

Editorial/project management: Lisa Plumridge with Laetitia Clapton
Copy editor: Paul Hines
Layout/DTP: Pat Hinsley & Alison Rayner
Proofreader: Yvonne Bergman

The publishers would like to thank the Ljubljana Tourist Board (LTB) and the following for supplying the copyright photographs for this book: Martin Belam, page 80; Christian MM Brady, page 36; Simon Krzic/Dreamstime.com, pages 1 & 99; Ljubljana Tourist Board, pages 5, 21, 59, 66 & 95; D Mladenovič/LTB, page 15; Ziga Okorn/Souhostel, page 39; Pictures Colour Library, pages 30 & 140; Slovenian Tourist Board (Archiv Postojnske jame, page 123; Bobo, page 49; B Kladnik, page 113; D Mladenovič, pages 47 & 119; J Skok/Slovenian Tourist Board, pages 40–1, 43 & 109); Meeli Tamm/pbase.com, page 16; D Wedam/LTB, pages 9, 13, 19, 63 & 65; Meghan Hurst, all others.

Send your thoughts to
books@thomascook.com

- Found a great bar, club, shop or must-see sight that we don't feature?
- Like to tip us off about any information that needs a little updating?
- Want to tell us what you love about this handy little guidebook and more importantly how we can make it even handier?

Then here's your chance to tell all! Send us ideas, discoveries and recommendations today and then look out for your valuable input in the next edition of this title.

Email the above address (stating the title) or write to: CitySpots Project Editor, Thomas Cook Publishing, PO Box 227, Coningsby Road, Peterborough PE3 8SB, UK.